DAVID SMITH

# *Be a Teacher*

## A MEMOIR IN TEN IDEAS

outskirts
press

Outskirts Press, Inc.
http://www.outskirtspress.com

Paperback ISBN: 978-1-4787-8571-2
Hardback ISBN: 978-1-4787-8572-9

Outskirts Press and the "OP" logo are trademarks belonging to Outskirts Press, Inc.

PRINTED IN THE UNITED STATES OF AMERICA

For
Janna, Peter, and Sadie,
who had the tough assignment
of living with me
while I was being a teacher

# TABLE OF CONTENTS

Foreword                                    i

1   Knowledge                               1

2   Decorum                                 22

3   Rigor                                   35

4   Humanity                                50

5   Play                                    68

6   Authority                               81

7   Patience                                95

8   Time                                    112

9   Books                                   125

10  Love                                    138

Acknowledgements                           151

# FOREWORD

More (Grimly): Be a teacher.
*A Man for All Seasons*

Grimly?

Sir Thomas More is speaking to a young man, Richard Rich, whom he recognizes as intellectually capable but morally weak. Rich wants More's help in launching a political career. More foresees the disasters likely to befall a corruptible spirit when it encounters the seductions of office. He urges Rich to accept instead an offered post as a school-master, extols the quiet life of the mind, admonishes him that "a man should go where he won't be tempted."

Rich isn't buying it. He admires More's elegant clothes. He sees that More is Councilor of England and will soon become Lord Chancellor, be outfitted with a heavy gold chain, entertain the King to dinner. Can a man striding along such a luminous career path credibly counsel others to retire from the limelight?

The inconsistency of his own position is what turns More grim. He himself—though for different reasons—is not perfectly suited for prominence. He knows it, knows that he may eventually lose his head for it, but cannot make himself turn aside. Perhaps he can at least save this plaintive and confused young fellow. Like a doctor advising the most desperate course of chemotherapy, he leans hard on his prescription.

Be a teacher.

No one ever told me to be a teacher. I came to the idea myself one spring morning in 1960, my junior year in boarding school. I was standing with friends under the portico of our enormous brick "cha-pel" (more like a cathedral), waiting for the bell that would summon us in for the daily 15-minute service. The service meant nothing to me, an incipient atheist, but when we sang a hymn I always enjoyed the way the organ made my breastbone resonate and the whole, vast, pillared and paneled interior of the place thrum with sound. We were required to be there and would be punished if we were not, but even without the coercion I might have showed up sometimes just for the grandeur. And since we *were* required, I could count on the companionship of the other boys, to whom I now heard myself announcing, without having planned on it at all, "I'm going to be an English teacher."

I said this not grimly but ecstatically, as if thick scales had just now fallen from my eyes and a thrilling vision had been revealed.

My friends did not seem particularly impressed. For one thing, seeming impressed was, among us, a weakness to be avoided; our cul-ture was founded firmly on an affectation of the blasé. For another, I had said nothing likely to impress my audience. Most of them, whether or not they had yet begun to set a definite course for themselves, would naturally be going into law, government, medicine, business, or invest-ment banking. They looked forward to moving ahead as soon as pos-sible into the world of success and authority, en route to which school was only a tedious way station. Why would anyone choose to remain permanently in such a backwater?

The bell clattered in its tower and we slipped through the closing doors into our seats. The organ rumbled; my sternum vibrated. I was happy, having settled my life. I had no opinion of the professions that my classmates would enter. In fact, I was so naïve that I barely knew these jobs existed and was completely unaware of their superior sta-tus. Later, when I did become aware of it, I was for a while pleasantly prone to believe that the *inferior* status of teaching—and the inferior income that it produced—made it more generous and more noble than other careers and to share More's doubtful premise that teachers are proof against corruption. A man should go where he won't be tempted, yes—but what more tempting than the smug myth of self-sacrificial purity?

But no moral calculus, self-deceiving or otherwise, was on my mind that morning, and very little intellectual calculus, either. I had always been a reader, had grown up in a family where books were as necessary and ubiquitous as food, and I was beginning to get interested in real literature; but the idea of passing down a tradition had no special appeal. What drew me to teaching was the same thing that drew me to chapel: the aesthetic of it, the drama. Of course I had had teachers who bored me stiff, lots of them, but I knew with the easy assurance of the ignorant and untried that I could do better than they did. The best ones, on the other hand, engaged me in a participatory theater that was entirely captivating. Dowdy in their dull suits, these men (and all my teachers *were* men) whom others might have dismissed as a troupe of chalk-stained wretches had for me an inexplicable radiance. I savored their witticisms, aped their mannerisms, speculated about their lives behind the scenes, regarded them as stars. And now, once I should serve a few years of apprenticeship that I hoped would pass quickly, I intended to become one of them.

In the event, I would become many of them, for the several very different schools I've taught in, the several decades of snarled American life that I've taught through, and the several stages of my own quest for self-definition have brought out different parts of me. A teacher, like a book being written, is a perpetual work in progress. He must publish every day when the bell rings, but he can still go back at night for revisions, can appear the next morning as a new edition of himself—and had better keep on doing so until he is too sclerotic to continue at all.

A couple of things that this book is not. It is not the story of a heroic teacher battling the entropy of impossible inner city schools. Teachers who have fought this fight have my enormous respect and admiration. All of my work has been in private independent schools, with mostly well-motivated students and at least reasonably supportive environments. And though I have enjoyed these advantages (or perhaps *because* I have enjoyed them?), I cannot claim to be telling the story of a teacher who, in the standard phrase, "changed his students' lives." Even if I had, that is a book that only my students would be qualified to write.

My vision of what it means to be a teacher has evolved continuously since that morning I decided to be one, but—despite one long moment of wavering—I have never regretted the choice. This book is the story of how becoming a teacher changed *my* life and of the teachers I became.

I set out to write a more or less conventional memoir but quickly found that the conventions did not quite suit my material. For one thing, my evolution, like that in the natural world, has been a curve twisted by contingency rather than a smooth, purposeful ascent. To present the story as a strict chronological narrative would be either to impose the graceful but distorting arc of well-made fiction or to bog down in the dead ends, digressions, and recursions of my teaching life as I have actually lived it. Then, too, ideas kept crowding in and elbowing the story-line aside, insisting—reasonably enough—that they, not plot points, should be at the core of a book in which the stakes are intellectual and the key moments play out in the mind.

Finally, I felt that the best way to represent my teaching life would be to fuse the two genres, memoir and essay, letting each assert itself when it would. The book is a *memoir in ideas*, with story and concept taking turns in the foreground. In the early chapters, where I aim to recreate the world that made me a teacher, the sequential story of my own schooling and the vivid personalities that carried it out predominate, and the ideas must content themselves with being heard as grace notes. In the later ones, less tied to particular times and places, theme takes center stage and the action comes from here and there as connections suggest themselves. What I have tried to avoid, however, is the kind of theoretical bubble-blowing that mars so much writing on education. My subject is not educational policy but educational experience, the daily work that goes on in a classroom. From page 1 on, readers will encounter real people, real successes and failures, real moments of elation and frustration. Without the emotional engagement, any picture of teaching would not just be incomplete: it would be empty at the center.

Ten ideas make up the bestiary of this book—ideas that I have been tracking since my first days in the classroom and that remain alive and elusive now that I have completed my fiftieth year of doing this work. What I think I know about my ten ideas keeps on shifting and shimmying even as I write; their evasiveness is what proves that they are interesting ideas and worth pursuing. In fact, the instability of knowledge—its subjectivity, its evanescence, and its often tenuous connection with the lives we lead—is a constant condition of a teacher's business and therefore an appropriate place to start a book on teaching. I begin, then, with the men in my family, none of whom worked in a school but all of whom were proud of what they knew and determined to teach me things; their headstrong pedagogy, no matter how much I sometimes tried to resist it and no matter how useless to them their own knowledge frequently seemed, is stamped in my DNA. I have learned more since, some of it even useful, but the Smith men, for better and for worse, are where everything began. And even now, many decades after the last of them made his final categorical assertion, they are still whispering in the back of my mind as I go about my work.

# Chapter 1

———— ∿∿ ————

# KNOWLEDGE

*MILTON ACADEMY, 2014. My senior English and American Lit class is stumped one morning by "The Charge of the Light Brigade." This chestnut has made the syllabus not for any literary merit but as an example of Victorian weltanschauung. Victorian weltanschauung is exactly what the kids don't get. They have attended diligently to years of lessons on rhetorical devices, and they are certain that they smell irony here. How could any poet actually intend to praise soldiers for making a suicidal cavalry charge, thousands of miles from anything they could have a personal stake in defending, at the behest of an incompetent hierarchy? The poem must be a send-up.*

*Part of my business as a teacher is to be clear with them: there can be no doubt that Tennyson meant everything he said about the quenchless honor of following orders straight into the jaws of death, sabering a Cossack or two, and then, if you're one of the few left in the saddle, riding back again. To let students leave the room in doubt as to this point would be to teach them nothing about the Victorian age.*

*The whispering Smith men counsel that I should put a quick spike in the irony hypothesis and move on. Your job, they say, is to scotch error as de-cisively as you can. (Being quasi-Victorians themselves, they are also ready to entertain the notion that a suicidal cavalry charge is a noble undertak-ing.) One of the useful things I have learned, however, is that what my students* do *know is at least as important as what they don't and is almost always a good place to start from. In this case, what they do know—in their marrow, though they were born years after the worst was over—is the whole wretched history of the twentieth century, its cruel misjudgments and casual, meaningless slaughters. They know that we've seen quite enough of men dribbling soccer balls through muddy wastelands under machine-gun fire and crawling blindly into tunnels booby-trapped with poison stakes. They know that we have to try to do better than that.*

*So, Yes, I say—"Yes" being the word that (as the Smith men never understood) a teacher must always try to find his way to. Yes, it is impor-tant to question the straightforwardness of any poetic voice. Yes, it is hard to imagine one's way into the mindset of 160 years ago. And yes, you're right—though Tennyson didn't mean it to be, "The Charge of the Light Brigade" ought* to *be ironic.*

My training in epistemology began at the family dinner table one evening in 1950, when I was six years old; and it began with a *No.*

There in the dining room of my grandparents' house in Carlisle, Pennsylvania, dinners were formal occasions, the places carefully set, candles lighted, my grandfather presiding, my grandmother at the foot of the table, later generations spread along the sides. As a child, I was hardly aware of the tensions that crisscrossed the room. I did know that a hand-lettered sign in the kitchen—"Margaret and Edith will eat anything"—registered the impatience my aunt and my mother felt for male tastes that ran repetitively to steak and potatoes. Once I had created a menu crisis myself when I helped to make a salad by dropping a whole peeled clove of garlic into the bowl and Granddaddy was naturally the one to bite into it. But of deeper lev-els of unease—the ongoing cold war between my grandmother and grandfather, my father's shame that, at 43, he and his wife and children still had to live with his parents—I as yet knew nothing. As the first grandchild in residence, I was growing up under a genial, indulgent sun, and neither the solemnity of the setting nor the shadows cast by family ghosts could stop me when I had a proclamation to make. Was I fueled by the hubris of some success at school that day? Did one of the adults' incessant hairsplitting semantic debates suggest an opening?

"I know all the words in the world," I announced, brazenly, into a moment of silence.

This verbal garlic clove did not call forth the outpouring of admiration that I expected. Genial sun or no, I could not be allowed to enjoy even for a moment such a monstrous self-delusion about a subject as important as language. Granddaddy and Daddy rose, beckoned for me to follow. We crossed the hall to the library. Granddaddy withdrew a book from one of the shelves, scanned the first page briefly, and presented it to me, his index finger stabbing a word that, I had to admit, I had never seen before.

I know more words now, having been an English teacher for fifty years, but I am still unsure what to make of the lesson that the Smith men felt duty bound to teach me that evening—a lesson, so they believed, in the sacred status of knowledge but one that also conveyed a darker collateral message about its repressive possibilities. Knowledge, we assume, is the coin of a teacher's realm, what separates the teacher from the taught—at least until he has done his job of passing it on across the generational divide. Yet knowledge, when we test it with our teeth, immediately reveals itself to be a suspect currency.

At six, as my boast showed, I not only understood the concept of knowledge in a basic way but had also begun to guess at the politics of it—that it was inseparable from politics. Knowledge, I knew, was something worth claiming, something that conferred status and perhaps power. As my elders were quick to point out, however, it was not something to be claimed lightly. The balance of power, the political calculus, was still decidedly in their favor.

Maybe, I now think, they were too quick to quash a prattling boy's enthusiasm and put him in his place. One can imagine families in which, when junior announces that he knows all the words in the world, grandfather replies, "Think of all the things you can say with them!" and lets it go at that. Does junior, as he then lies in bed, indulge himself in reprehensible fantasies of omniscience and omnipotence? Or does he dreamily reach for some of the words that hover at the limits of his grasp and juggle them until they fall into a poem that he can recite to his pillow?

As conceived by the men in the Smith household in the years after World War II, knowledge—especially knowledge of words—was hard-edged stuff, weapons-grade material not to be fooled with. It was also something that the young lacked and the old had and were charged with handing down. They did not stop to think very much about the long-term utility of it, whether it contributed in any intrinsic way to living well. Happy or not—and they seem to have been unhappy much of the time—they knew what they knew and staked their identities on it; and they never hesitated to let you know what you didn't know.

In fact, all the Smith men in the generations just before mine had missed their calling. They were teachers—old-school teachers—by temperament and inclination but not by profession. My grandfather, Paul, was a chemist and engineer. When my family lived with him in the late 1940's, he was working for the C. H. Masland carpet company in Carlisle, developing a machine to make durable pile carpeting for the floors of cars. My father, Sidney, collaborated on the project with him, and we all lived together in a large and even somewhat stately brick house on South Hanover Street, not far from the courthouse that still showed the pockmarks of rebel cannonballs fired during the advance on Gettysburg. My uncle Carleton, the second son, had married a rich woman and was leading the life of a gentleman farmer in Bucks County, 90 miles away.

Designing carpet machines and raising steers for market were good, practical, money-making enterprises that suited men who had lived straight through the Depression without a lot of margin. "I hope you haven't deceived Edith," my grandfather wrote to my father shortly after my parents' wedding in 1941, "as to the fact that she was marrying into a family which has been extremely poor for a number of years, and isn't far from it right now." In another letter of the time, he calculated that he and his sons had a combined income of $800 a month and therefore should be able to spare $25 a month to keep afloat his wife's maiden sisters, Cora and Lil, who were being neglected by their closer kin. If each son could come up with $6, he would muster the other $13. It sounds like a near thing.

My grandfather's Harvard degrees (he had earned both a Bachelor's and a Master's) had not been a ticket to success. Instead, starting out shortly after the turn of the century, he had found his way into a series of research and development jobs for companies that tended to fire their staffs when a particular project ended. The family had rattled around from Delaware to Rhode Island to Texas to Vermont to upstate New York, never staying anywhere long enough to get comfortable. Their nomadic life had become a settled grievance for my Texan grandmother, Maud (known to me as Gaga), whose disappointed expectations of recreating the Tara-esque southern lifestyle that she liked to believe she had known as a child set up a steady toxic undercurrent in the household. Gaga radiated disdain for everyone and everything in Carlisle. Neighbors, tradesmen, and people in the street were all "common as pigs' tracks" to her way of thinking. Her own story blended in her mind with the tragic failure of the Confederacy, and she spent a lot of time brooding aloud about the heirlooms that had been put into storage and ruined or lost during the family's long years in the wilderness. Resentment that did not find its way into words expressed itself as headaches, shingles, conjunctivitis, and an ongoing need for expensive dental work.

Whatever the actual deprivations and despite the fact that Gaga had no interest at all in the life of the mind, the family had usually found money for the sons' education. Both of them graduated from boarding school and entered Harvard. My father came within a semester of finishing, then dropped out, for reasons that were never spoken about in my hearing but at a minimum reflected a deep reluctance to step from the academy into the waiting world of responsibility, where knowledge could no longer be appreciated as a pure aesthetic pleasure but actually had to be applied. Carleton completed a single semester. His official reason for quitting was that the family fortunes had cratered with the stock market and they could, at last, no longer afford the tuition. He went into the restaurant business, then somehow surfaced during the war as an efficiency expert for the Sperry Gyroscope Company, where he was said to have taken a manufacturing process in which some parts traveled 17 miles from far-flung warehouses and reduced it to an assembly line 186 feet long. (He was also said to have been the most even-tempered man in the company—always angry.) My father, who had majored in English, retooled as a self-taught mechanical engineer. In the 30's, the market for moony self-taught mechanical engineers was little better than the market for moony former English majors, and when he couldn't attach himself to one of the shifting family enterprises, he often went hungry.

In hard times, when there may or may not be bread on the table, what you *know* is something you can count on, a nest egg safely locked away from even the worst of circumstances. The danger is that, being overvalued, it may lose the pliancy that genuine knowledge must have and stiffen into a belligerent personal orthodoxy. I started my own work life in the flusher second half of the 20th century and have never myself needed to wonder where the next paycheck might be coming from (though, in accord with the value that our society places on its teachers, the checks were often small). My "hard times" were not financial but professional, and I cringe today when I think of how, in my early days as a teacher, I tried vainly to cover my ignorance of the craft with strident assertiveness that had been modeled for me in my childhood.

For the Smith men, pontificating was not only a way to salve the sting of living in the wilderness but also a pleasant pastime. They enjoyed lecturing even more than drinking (though the two were often concurrent); and the fact that the sons' formal educations had been cut short only amplified the vehemence of their pronouncements. Listening to them was a lesson not only in the vast areas of learning about which they considered themselves experts—matters as diverse as astronomy, Wagnerian opera, internal combustion engines, English and French grammar, and the fine points of political science—but also in a whole style of discourse. Samuel Johnson's idea of "talking for victory" was the order of the day in our house, and words were the halberds that would hew a path through enemy ranks. Alternative styles—talking to learn, talking to elucidate—would eventually become the essence of what I understood as teaching, but back then they never had a chance. Back then we talked to *win*. My claim, at six, to be an unabridged dictionary was an early indication that I had assimilated the family male culture; and the stern immediacy with which my elders refuted it just confirmed that conversation was a contest—one that ended when knowledgeable winners put ignorant losers to rout, or at least when the more assertive pounded the less so into submission.

In my long-running and still incomplete efforts to rid myself of this poisonous premise, I have benefited from the inspiration of the family *female* culture. Aunt Margaret, after 30 years with Paul, Sidney, and Carleton, had refined her strategies of resistance. She and my mother operated as a guerilla army, harrying the flanks of the patriarchy as targets of opportunity presented themselves, challenging not only the men's monochrome diet but also their pretensions to infallibility. When the air in the house got too professorial, Margaret (and her droll boyfriend Angus, who was instinctively aligned with the female side) sometimes just packed up my sister and me for a drive into rolling Pennsylvania farmland. Dueling with cornstalks, racing sticks under a bridge, trying to keep up with the errant cocker spaniel Coco, we were relieved to learn that there was more to life than having all the answers. Now, when I find myself inclined to pontificate, I think of how Margaret would have relished a mischievous remark someone made about graduates of the French *Grandes Ecoles*, a prestigious post-university program for aspiring members of the power elite: "They know everything," the saying went. "Unfortunately, they don't know anything else."

The Smith men were not frauds, however. They knew things haphazardly and by halves, but they were genuinely interested in the things they knew and they genuinely valued knowledge. The trouble was that they never managed to unify their extensive collection of factual fragments into a successful philosophical system. They scored points, but they did not attain to wisdom.

The classical languages were at the core of any liberal arts education when my grandfather went to school in the 1890's, and he had taken Greek at Andover from a teacher named "Zeus" Benner. When I got there, 60 years later, Benner no longer occupied his place on Olympus and was remembered only because his name had been given to the building that housed the campus snack bar; the classics themselves had begun to seem a little dusty. Granddaddy, too, had certainly forgotten most of what Benner had taught him, dactylic hexameters being of little use in the carpet business. Still, he would occasionally rumble something about "rosy-fingered dawn," and he once recounted with great emotion the delirious cheers of the Greek troops in the *Anabasis* when, completing their long withdrawal from the barbarian hinterland, they caught their first glimpse of the sea: "Thalassa! Thalassa!" He may have felt by then that his own life had been a similarly harassed retreat through hostile territory. What he knew was a tag from ancient history; what he didn't know and had never known was how to wring some residual sweetness from the disappointments of living.

*Look who thinks he just hiked home from Persia,* my wife (a late but well-armed recruit to the band of family female partisans) would have said to him if she had been there. And it is true that the intellectual preoccupations of the Smith men often served as stalking horses for their more romantic or melodramatic self-conceptions. Perhaps because they had listened to Gaga for so long, these self-conceptions tended to revolve around noble but lost causes, flags in the dust.

For my grandfather, his marriage itself was one of these. I know this not only through family oral history but also because he put it in writing. The relationship had begun, in 1903, with a burst of mutual adoration so bright that it still seems to singe the pages of the courtship letters, an immense bundle of which survives. The sentences stagger under the weight of interjected endearments. She is "my heart's treasure," "my precious," "my darling sweetheart," and (jumping the gun) "my sweet, true bride"; he is "darling mine," "my very life," and "my own true noble husband." Neither of the young people seems to have had the slightest suspicion that they were profoundly unsuited to each other in both intellect and temperament.

By 1941, the correspondence had darkened considerably. Paul and Maud lived apart most of that year, she in Cambridge, New York, he in a hotel in Rockford, Illinois, where the prototype of the carpet machine was being fabricated. "I realize only too well now that I am not the kind of person you should have married," he writes, "and that I have not lived up to your expectations of me." A neatly typed and carbon-copied *cri de coeur*, the letter goes on for four pages. He reminds her that the Masland project is a last miraculous chance to attain the comfort that has eluded them, assures her that he has "never been your enemy in any sense of the word," points out that they are both 60 years old and perhaps have little time left, begs her to set aside her animosity for him and come to Rockford so that they can begin anew. And he gives her—this part he can be sure of—detailed instructions on what trains to take and how to handle her baggage.

At one point he also notes that she has described his letters as "full of long, involved sentences which don't mean anything." In fact, though they do register as somewhat rhetorical, their style is direct and forceful, the language that of someone trying with the honesty of utter desperation to get a grip on experience that is burning his hands like a runaway rope. The complacent certitudes of a Harvard man no longer avail; he sees that he must stretch himself for a new kind of knowledge, a new way of applying it. And this particular letter worked, to an extent. Maud did catch "The Wolverine" out of Albany at 9:00 p.m. and they lived together, uneasily, for the remainder of his life. The carpet machine, put on hold during the war while the company converted to manufacturing tarpaulins, eventually also worked, to an extent. It began to produce carpet, but of a type no longer required by the forward-looking Maslands. One evening in 1951, Granddaddy was returning from the drugstore with a prescription for Gaga when he stumbled and broke his hip on the sidewalk in front of the house. We watched anxiously through the parted curtains of the living room as the ambulance arrived. His final decline had begun, and he was dead within two years.

My father, being the dreamiest of the three Smith men by a large margin, took their love of lost causes the farthest. In a lost cause he recognized emotionally safe terrain, experience packed away in a past where active engagement was no longer possible and therefore imposed no irritating practical demands. As he grew more and more sedentary in his middle years, he read obsessively in the history of adventure, with special attention (as a college course catalogue might say) to catastrophic endings. Like most of us, he sought knowledge that would support his already established world-view. Stories of mountaineers who vanished into the mist and the last thoughts of Antarctic explorers as the wind howled and the relief party blundered off the track spoke straight to his vivid sense of personal doom. Reminiscing about the 1927 Lindbergh flight, he recalled not the glorious landing in Paris but the melancholy, foreboding voice of the radio announcer who reported the takeoff—how the tiny, overloaded plane struggled to lift itself from the runway and then disappeared over the vast and empty Atlantic. Better for Lindy, perhaps, if he and the *Spirit of St. Louis* had gone down without a trace rather than having to endure that vulgar, triumphant fuss at Le Bourget.

Melancholia is a close cousin to sentimentality, and the Smith men's knowledge, objective though they liked to imagine it, was vividly tinged with sentiment. Carleton, who prided himself on being tough-minded, usually in contrast to whatever family member he felt was thinking most fecklessly at the moment, nevertheless became plain mawkish when he spoke of the old days at Andover. He never said a word about any idea that he had been asked to consider there, but the japes and pranks, the solidarity of boys against masters, the intoxication of school spirit all got him going like nothing else in the decades since he had graduated in the class of 1930. He kept in his study a framed 8x10 yearbook photo of his roommate, Doc Purney, on which Doc had inscribed a famous line from the *Aeneid*, one uttered at a point when the hero and his companions are in the most desperate straits: *Perhaps, someday, we will take pleasure in remembering even this.* Even this!—the convention that boarding school was a life of shared suffering rather than of irresponsible and frivolous youthful ease must already have seemed transparently false to them while they lived it. In any case, Carleton did look back with pleasure—on handsome Doc, on the patriarchal headmaster Al Stearns, and even on the encounter with a hockey puck that had left an inch-long scar on his chin when he was playing for the Big Blue at Boston Garden.

I met Doc Purney years later when he and Carleton came up for their 45th reunion while I was teaching at the school. Having admired the photo and the apparent intensity of the bond between them, I was disappointed to find not only that Doc had nothing to say to me, though I was now a custodian of the place that had given him the happiest unhappy days of his life, but also that he and Carleton had nothing to say to each other and took no pleasure in remembering anything. At this point, even the imaginary past was no longer sustaining, and the de-contextualized literary shred that had once looked like useful knowledge had lost its power to invoke a believable narrative. They were not interested either in their shared history or in the way the school was evolving into its own future. Instead, they got plastered, skipped the seminars on Andover Today and even the get-togethers with their all-too-mutable classmates, and went home.

In the 1950's, when I was growing up, Carleton became my model of a man, an exemplar of *savoir faire*: he not only knew things but knew how to make things happen, how to shorten assembly lines that the rest of the family seemed content to let stretch on indefinitely. The Bucks County farm—a hundred acres, two houses, and a barn—that he and his wife Martha had bought after the war with money she brought into the marriage was an expression of his exacting tastes and his active will to perfect. He set out to live beautifully on it and, for a time at least, established it as an object lesson in the differences between the ordinary and the excellent. In my dining room today hangs a painting, by a well-known local water-colorist, that shows the two of them having breakfast on their terrace sometime around 1955. Early sunlight sifts through the enormous trees of the yard and flecks with gold the walls of the house. The couple at the breakfast table, seen from a distance that eliminates individual characteristics, appear to be icons of gentility suspended in boundless peace.

It is easy enough to recognize now the fault lines that ran through and under this impression of grace. The painting has the illusive glow of an ideal course—the course that exists in the teacher's mind before students arrive to take its perfectly calculated message in a hundred different directions and misdirections. Carleton, as it turned out, knew no more than his father about how to lead a consistently happy life. Already he and Martha and their friends were drinking steadily from late afternoon to midnight almost every day, and if for the time being their livers could take it, the structure of their lives could not. A fling at the construction business with Martha's capital—high-end homes for rusticators from New York and Philadelphia—began hopefully, produced three or four houses that did sell, then foundered in a bitter falling out with Carleton's partner and a substantial loss. Terry, Carleton's son by a previous marriage, came to stay with them but took a hunting knife to some of the furniture and had to be sent back to his mother in Louisiana. Later, in a further and this time all but unforgivable disgrace, he entered and was almost immediately expelled from Andover as well. Carleton himself moved out and set up housekeeping with a woman in New Hope for a few months before he came creeping home. When not working his way through one of these scrapes, he didn't have enough to do and would entertain himself by sparring ineffectually with the nature around him. He dammed the creek to make a swimming hole, but it quickly silted up. From the terrace, he blasted away with a .20-.20 at woodchucks on the far hillside. Though the ostensible purpose of this barrage was to keep the steers from breaking their legs in the woodchuck holes, it went on well after Carleton had quit the cattle business. Like a trooper in the Light Brigade, he kept charging well past the point of obvious futility. A good shot, he probably hit some of the woodchucks, but, woodchuck reproduction being what it is, he never got ahead.

If we were rational in our choice of idols, there would be no point in idolatry, and Carleton would probably not have made the A-list. But we take what's out there and ask our imaginations to do the rest. I idolized him. After Terry flamed out, I often spent weeks on end at the farm in the summer. My official role was lawn boy, and Carleton, embracing his post as mentor and pedant, insisted that I study for the part. The text was a *Reader's Digest* story about a lawn boy who painstakingly learned the difference between a $3 job and a $5 job. (The $5 job involved cross-cutting for a neater appearance and clipping by hand around the edges of the perennial borders so as not to decapitate any prize blooms.) Though I never attained perfection, I served the turn and came to like mowing. The perfume of cut grass and gasoline was a tonic, the countryside stretched away invitingly in all directions, the sun started honest sweat, and there was an endless supply of Cokes in the back hall to lubricate the breaks that I took more or less on my own schedule. Best of all was the patterned beauty the mower imposed, grass sheared even and bent to catch the light in orderly alternating stripes, like the diamond at Connie Mack Stadium. As a 12-year-old I would not have said, "This is beautiful"; but I felt it and was pleased to have a part in creating it.

Since the lawn needed mowing only once a week, plenty of time remained for my unofficial role, which was to be the student of Carleton's world-view, his adamantine sense of how things are or should be. In addition to the value of honest sweat, this included some precepts about the relations of men and women (necessary, but inevitably tense if not outright antagonistic) and about the fundamental skills of a *bon vivant* (how to tie a bow tie). Often on a summer evening, Carleton, Martha, and I would dress up and go out for a restaurant meal. A favorite spot was Colligan's Inn in Stockton, New Jersey, where we ate outside on a terrace. The inn had been immortalized by Richard Rogers in the song "There's a small hotel with a wishing well..." The wishing well, the candlelight, the stars, the snap and sizzle of the service created a heady aura for me. My own family never ate in restaurants unless we were on a trip--and then it would be a downscale mom-and-pop place with bready meatloaf and instant mashed potatoes. Not only was the food better at Colligan's, but Carleton knew how to command the scene in a way that my father never did. He greeted the maitre d', Toby, with a suave combination of warmth and authority, gave exacting instructions on the preparation of martinis and steaks, signaled for the bill with a tiny hand flick that suggested he had the waiter on the end of a string. Years later, when I watched the opening of *Schindler's List* and saw Oscar Schindler playing the high-roller at the nightclub in Krakow, I felt that he and Carleton might have been brothers.

I did not always feel that Carleton and my father were brothers, though they looked much alike. My favorite photo of them appears to have been taken sometime around 1940—two handsome young men in suits with white shirts and ties neatly held in place by collar pins, they are standing on a lawn somewhere with bare, March-looking trees in the background. Exactly equal in height and with identical builds and the same long faces and high foreheads that my grandfather had passed on to them along with so many of his attitudes, they both smile faintly straight into the camera and at first glance register as brothers all the way. But to a knowing eye their differences are apparent. Carleton adopts an insouciant posture, hands in his pockets, and his expression, though friendly, conveys the hint of a warning: don't tread on me. Dad folds his hands defensively in the crotch area, and there is a deferential tilt to his head, accentuated by a narrow, Chaplinesque mustache and a stray forelock that one can imagine him tugging at if he were to come and ask a superior for a favor. He is the older brother but not the alpha one.

Growing up, I felt myself poised uneasily between the two kinds of knowledge that Dad and Carleton represented to me. I aspired to Carleton's seemingly confident assumption of real-world command but recognized that my natural affinity was for Dad's book-learning, which unfortunately seemed to come in a package with self-effacing weakness. Driving one day from Carleton's house to ours, Dad and I came to a construction site on the highway. Amid the dust and the lumbering machines, only one lane remained open. My father slowed to a crawl, then stopped. We sat there for a few seconds. Then one of the workers walked over impatiently to wave us through. I don't remember what he said, but the expression on his face and the tone of his voice were unmistakable: *Stop daydreaming and get the hell out of our way.* Dad could undoubtedly have explained exactly how roads are built, but there he sat in the middle of this one, blocking traffic.

The popular culture that was flexing its considerable post-war muscles around us in the early 50's galled my father into a quiet elitist frenzy. Like guys driving graders and moving tons of earth, it made him feel puny and insignificant, and he responded by becoming a crank (though to all appearances a highly conventional one). The one space where he could set his own cranky standards was his family. For a long time he forbade my sister and me to read comic books. Though this ban was eventually lifted, it had, in the meantime, the effect of most bans, which was to make the banned object emit a fascinating radiance. Once, when we visited the home of older cousins who had since gone on to high school and college, we discovered a hideout that they had maintained in an old barn. Except for a couple of funky mattresses, the only furnishings were thousands of comic books. We could not have been happier if we had stumbled on a treasure cave.

At home we were at last permitted the occasional comic, but there was no TV. All through my early years of grade school, the lack of this necessary appliance made me a desperate outcast, cut off from the shared knowledge that bound others into a club. Before school and at recess, I wandered alone among classmates who were still in rapture, 12 hours after the fact, over seeing cowboys shot down in the street, detectives closing the jaws of justice on punks and thugs.

"Aw, did you see *Hopalong Cassidy* last night?"

"Aw, did you see *Dragnet*?"

My ears burned with it--especially the "aw," which functioned as a preliminary exclamation point for questions of special urgency. I lowered my head and kept walking. This deprivation, piled as it was on other trials of childhood, seemed particularly cruel. By fourth grade I was already the class intellectual, the kid who could read better than anyone else and whose cerebral tendencies were complemented, as cerebral tendencies often seemed to be, by ineptness and incompetence in the practical sphere. Here in school, where the acquisition of knowledge was supposed to be primary, knowledge of the kind that was valued at home didn't help and was even faintly embarrassing. My vocabulary made no difference when I lost my baseball cards, piles at a time, to people who could flip more accurately. Playing flag football in gym class, even the boy with the game leg and the orthopedic shoe could leave me in his uneven tracks. Still, if I had known enough to talk credibly about *Dragnet*, I might have been able to hang on to some shreds of self-respect.

Fortunately, everyone else in the neighborhood had a television, and I roamed from house to house, a beggar of moving images. My chief benefactor was Millie Grogan, who lived in the big stone mansion adjacent to ours. A generous and naïve soul, Millie was easily impressed by mental activity of any sort; and because she had no children of her own, she found my precocities particularly winning. I would lecture her, Smith-fashion, on the technology of space travel, shamelessly basing my presentation on ideas I had picked up from the science fiction novels that I read by the dozen or from *Mechanix Illustrated* at the barbershop. As far as she was concerned, I might as well have been tenured at M.I.T. She let me have unlimited use of their tube.

The stuff I watched on it was a robustly idiotic pot pourri running from Howdy Doody to Willy the Worm and culminating each afternoon in *Atom Squad*, which appeared in a miniseries format of five fifteen-minute installments a week. *Atom Squad* had a stirring title sequence, with music that I can still play back in my head and men in hazmat suits moving murkily through a shattered landscape. The plots were standard Cold War nightmares in which Commissar Brusilov and his Red underlings schemed to irradiate the Free World.

If Dad had seen this drivel, he probably would have embargoed the Grogans' television, too—and also given me a point by point rundown on the absurdities of *Atom Squad's* pseudo-science. But my after-school video forays ended before he returned from work at Sperry Rand in Philadelphia, where he had become part of the team developing the primitive, chattering high-speed printers that were to capture data from the first generation of Sperry computers. As a pioneer in the knowledge explosion, he dealt with small, definite things that could be flattened onto blueprints, a realm well suited to his fussy, precise, and deliberate personality. How machine parts would click together with other machine parts was something you could know. The curves of the human body and the unpredictable alarms and excursions of human emotional life were difficult territory for him. His work clothes— heavy tweed suits and gunboat-sized wing-tip shoes—made him seem substantial, but he took no pleasure in physicality. Under the tweeds, he was lanky, almost gaunt.

Though high-speed printing was his métier, Dad hated to be hurried. The harder the rest of us strained at the leash, the more likely he was to produce his favorite adage, "Let's not get ahead of ourselves." Fussiness was for him not a quirk but a survival strategy, enabling him to paper over the abyss with minutiae. After my mother prevailed on him to give up cigarettes, he smoked a pipe, which required an elaborate ritual of reaming, tamping, and flaring that slowed everything down and buffered him against intrusive stimuli. I was often frustrated by my inability to get him to pick up the pace, but I also benefited from his unusual patience—a quality that I lacked myself and later, when I saw that teaching would be impossible without it, had to work hard to cultivate. Dad's kindness was part failure to engage, but it was indisputably kindness. Casting for bass from a lakeside dock on our annual two-week vacations to Cooperstown, I would neglect to brake the old-fashioned reel with my thumb, so that when the lure hit the water the line would rush ahead and pile up in a horribly tangled backlash. "That's really a bad one," was all Dad would say. Then he would pick the thicket apart. For half an hour or more, as evening fell and his own fishing time evaporated, he would work out every knot and kink. Today, addressing myself to the maddening convolutions of thought in a student's paper, I often think admiringly of Dad's way with a backlash.

When we were at home with no backlashes to unsnarl, he read to us almost every night. First came the sentimental nature stories of Thornton W. Burgess; eventually we graduated to Conan Doyle, whose Holmes stories Dad relished. The lessons that Holmes taught Watson might also prove useful to my sister and me, who needed to learn that a frame of reference is necessary in order to convert raw sense data into useful knowledge: *You see, Watson, but you do not observe.* (If only my father and the other Smith men, Watsons so much of the time, had been able to bring this principle more successfully to bear on their own lives!) Doyle's plot turns occasioned mini-lectures on history and science. When Dr. Grimesby Roylott in a fit of pique bent Holmes's poker in half and Holmes calmly straightened it, Dad paused to explain why the work-hardening of iron made Holmes's feat much the greater. That the cerebral Holmes could muster such impressive physical force probably pleased Dad's cerebral self. Still more often there were breaks to gloss unfamiliar or interesting words or to admire ones that fell into their contexts with the perfect combination of inevitability and surprise. Thirty years later, lying in a hospital bed after a collapse that had snuffed out almost all his long-term and short-term memory, he could still finish sentences in Twain's *Roughing It* when I came in one night to read to *him*. The Twain party blasted away at a "jackass rabbit," which took off for San Francisco at high speed.

"Long after he was out of sight--," I read.

"--we could hear him whiz," my father completed, leaning on the "whiz." A few minutes later he sank back into dopey sleep.

All the Smith men focused much of their intellectual energy and much of their fussiness on language. Like many people of indeterminate class, they held hard to whatever markers of superiority were available to them. No matter how much they might be struggling to make ends meet, they always believed that they knew the difference between the right way and the wrong way to *say* something. Prescriptivism was their approach to grammar as to almost everything else. Carleton railed for years about violations of pronoun case. Apparently he was surrounded by people who, with no evident shame, said things like "They invited Jerry and I to dinner." When I took a linguistics course in graduate school and learned that the function of linguists was to describe rather than to dictate, I got into a heated dispute with him. By then (1967 or so, with the lessons of *Reader's Digest* long behind us and the conflict of generations in full swing), he found me politically suspect and could hardly bear to see me raising the flag of revolutionary gibberish alongside that of the Comintern. What would the world be like, he wanted to know, if we just made up all the rules as we went along? I didn't have the wit to tell him, as one of my own students much later told me, that if language purists had had their way we'd all still be speaking in grunts. Eventually he simmered down, but at the end of the evening he could not refrain from a final thrust. I was going to drive back to Wisconsin the next day. Seizing one of the boxes that I had stacked in the kitchen, he asked, with the air of a lawyer shooting home the last bolt in his closing argument, "Can me help you load the car?"

Dad's crotchets in this field were at least as ferocious. His customary mildness left him altogether when he felt that words were being abused. He scorned the mutation of nouns into verbs and would gag ostentatiously if he heard someone say, "I gifted my friend with a necktie." Fifty years before George W. Bush began slaughtering the word in mendacious warnings about Iraq's weapons of mass destruction, President Eisenhower's pronunciation of "nuclear" as "nuke-ular" would drive Dad into paroxysms of highbrow contempt. He was a registered Republican at the time but could not abide poor Ike's assaults on the mother tongue. What he thought about the thousands of A-bombs that were poised to obliterate the planet he never said: "nuke-ular" was atrocity enough. Once, on parents' night at my middle school, he noticed that someone had written "SHIT" on a blackboard. He later asked me whether the word was in common use by my peers, and I disingenuously assured him that it was not. The answer seemed to satisfy him. He did not ask and presumably did not want to know how I felt about the ongoing cruelties and humiliations of middle school life, a topic on which I might have spoken at length if I had been in the habit of discussing reality with him. Reality was not something he liked to discuss. To him, words were ends in themselves, and all the more fascinating and beautiful for being free of any pedestrian duty to signify.

"Words won't save you," my wife says now when I am trying to talk my way out of some untenable position. I know she is right, but I can't quite eradicate the hope that somehow, for once, they will; and for this wishful thinking—for a stubborn sense that words do matter, even if they yield no immediate practical payoff—I have the Smith men to thank. I must thank them, too, for their strenuous efforts to teach me what they thought they knew, efforts that planted the germ of the idea that I might become a teacher. To become what I now think of as a *good* teacher, I had to set aside many of the lessons that they intentionally and unintentionally taught. Talking for victory, for example, though always tempting, is not what good teachers do. Knowing everything is not a substitute for knowing some other important things.

# Chapter 2

———— ❧ ————

# Decorum

*GRANT SWARTLEY, SEVENTH-GRADE math teacher, folds his brown suit jacket neatly over the back of a chair and clambers atop his classroom desk. To me, his lugubrious, jowly face and stocky build suggest no particular age; he is just another adult, somewhere between 30 and 60, and the rudimentary algebra he teaches us is a dreary business, a number-shuffle not too difficult to master but lacking any inherent interest or purpose. In this somnolent year lost in the middle of a somnolent decade, we sleepwalk through it, as we do almost everything academic.*

*Swartley, however, is reputed to have one distinctive talent, which he will now put on display. For weeks, the boys who have seen it before have been begging for his rooster imitation. As a relative newcomer to Meadowbrook School, I haven't experienced the spectacle myself, but it seems a pleasant alternative to another round of factoring, and I am as happy as anyone when this time, instead of issuing a coy demurral, he strips down and climbs into position. Headmaster Shuttleworth, a dour, inhibiting figure, has left the building for lunch and the time is right.*

*Having committed himself by mounting the desk, Swartley does not hesitate. Tucking a thumb in each armpit to create two stubby wings, he jerks his elbows three or four times, crows lustily, and leaps, necktie flapping, to the floor. The room explodes in applause. Bruce Dunham and Selden Gates, whose relentless nagging has finally paid off, are doubled over with laughter. Eventually we get back to work, after a fashion; but this one concentrated moment of subversive hilarity seems to make up for many days of plodding.*

That order must reign in a classroom is one of the oldest premises in the teaching profession and has often attracted into it the Shuttleworths of the world, men and women who missed their calling as drill sergeants. No doubt these people took it as a matter of course that they themselves must never break step while in front of the troops, and probably the idea that it might be fun and even effective to cut an unexpected jig once in a while didn't even occur to most of them. Though the truth is that education as often resembles the helter-skelter retreat of Napoleon's Grande Armée from Moscow as its highly-organized and purposeful advance, teachers of this sort insist on maintaining the fiction that they are overseeing a parade-ground review.

Today, the military science of teaching and learning leans heavily on what are called Best Practices, a set of precepts that tend to be as intuitively obvious (and difficult to implement in the field) as "seize the high ground" or "secure your flanks" but that our leaders expound as the product of rarefied and exacting research and as a recipe for the kind of perfection that, in the sweat and static of a real classroom, can never be achieved. When, as inevitably happens, Best Practices aren't getting the job done, an appeal to experience against such rock-ribbed authority is liable to be dismissed as merely "anecdotal"—the idiosyncratic plaint of a flat-earther or global-warming skeptic. After centuries of improvisation and benighted groping, we now, it seems, are lucky enough to *know* what Best Practices are, though their high degree of abstraction makes them more useful to those who are trying to assert administrative presence than to those tasked with operating at the platoon level. We may still wonder, for example, whether Swartley's barnyard moment meets any of the criteria. When Horace, in 10 B. C. E., articulated Best Practices for the theater, he explicitly proscribed the showy and the sensational: "Medea must not butcher her children in the presence of the audience, nor the monstrous Atreus cook his dish of human flesh within public view... I shall turn in disgust from anything of this kind that you show me." That my 7th-grade math class (an unsophisticated audience, to be sure) turned toward the unabashedly showy rooster jump in delight is evidence that Best Practices are in the mind of the beholder.

Before I came to Meadowbrook in the fall of 1955, none of my teachers had ever staged such a flagrant breach of decorum or even showed a flash of what could be thought of as personality. The dominant message had been that although we might be learning to square dance in gym class or constructing a model Thanksgiving turkey out of a potato, toothpicks, and colored paper, school was a rather sober business, a place where, teacher or student, one stayed between the lines. At Franklin School in Carlisle, a grim brick bastion from the 19th century, a wooden slat hung beneath the chalk tray in each room. We believed that these were used for paddling the recalcitrant, but in fact they were probably just rulers, for despite the building's jail-like appearance, the days of corporal punishment were long gone, replaced by gentler methods. My first-grade teacher, Miss Clark, exuded a bland sweetness even when she was letting me know that I should desist from poking a pencil eraser into the wide open and receptive mouth of the girl beside me— my earliest certain memory of a schoolroom. Her colleagues could have stepped straight from a nearby bank or insurance agency. One of them, Mr. Williams, had features that suggested the promising sobriquet "Old Needle-Nose," and that is what, as my taste for character began to develop, I tried calling him behind his back, in hopes of generating a little narrative; but he disappointingly failed to respond to my efforts with any rich Dickensian behavior. Mrs. Moyer, a circuit-riding art teacher who turned up once a week, marked Halloween by instructing us to remember that "Mrs. Moyer very rarely uses black" as she slashed broad bands of black watercolor across a picture of a witch in flight. This early example of do-as-I-say-not-as-I-do teaching struck me as funny, and I regaled my family with it. But Mrs. Moyer was not around enough to register as anything more than a passing anecdote, and her ambivalence about transgressing her own boundaries suggested that the boundaries, not the transgression, were the point.

Meadowbrook might have seemed to be another unlikely field for idiosyncratic characters. A K-8 boys' day school in a moderately snooty part of suburban Philadelphia, it had begun life just after World War I with the sure hand of the Reverend Dr. John Walker at the helm. Walker had retired 14 years before my arrival, supposedly when he noticed that the students were beginning to be able to outrun him on the track; but his portrait still dominated the main hallway, radiating probity, and he himself remained rector of the nearby Huntingdon Valley Chapel and a sainted presence in the background of the school—too righteous to meddle, but so righteous that he meddled without even trying. (Rector as in rectangle: the guy who makes sure that all the corners are square.) The place was nominally non-sectarian but Episcopalian to the core.

Perhaps the presumption of decorum was so strong that it actually created a little space for non-conformity; or perhaps, in a middle school, all decorum is pretense, an illusory dance-floor over a mudwrestling pit. In *The Coup*, John Updike writes about an African bureaucrat busily spinning a web of imaginary authority, and every middle school experience I've been involved in, on both sides of the table, has been just this sort of delicate, mutually understood convention: *You pretend to be in charge and we'll pretend to obey you.* In any case, Swartley's rooster jump was not the only unbuttoning of personality at Meadowbrook. On my first day at school (I had hardly slept in my terror about making what educators breezily refer to as "the transition"), my classmates warned me to stay on the right side of "Hurricane Harry" Maloney, a young English teacher with bulging eyes and a tendency to raise his voice in moments of choler. Staying on the right side of teachers had always been easy enough for me, and the boys themselves, with their clubby insider knowledge and crowding bodies encased in maroon and gray Meadowbrook sweaters, were more threatening than any teacher could have been. In the event, I never saw Maloney get above Force 8 on the Beaufort Scale. But unlike any teacher I had encountered before, he actually seemed to enjoy our company and would stand around with us at recess, trying out terms from the lexicon of rock-and-roll and commenting sardonically on the literary deficiencies of the Mickey Spillane novels that he for some reason thought we were reading on our own time.

Swartley did not crow again in my presence but he did once send us into hysterics by offering to diagram the layout of his back yard and then sketching on the blackboard what was unmistakably the outline of a woman's breasts and hips. Again Dunham and Gates, who were bigger and more developed than the rest of us, especially me, led the merriment. My own laughter struck a slightly false note. Though I had known plenty of girls in public school and had even had a putative girl friend there, puberty seemed more like a slightly sinister mystery than a joke. I laughed only because I didn't want to be left out.

Despite these flashes of color, the official palette at Meadowbrook was monochrome. Banks and insurance agencies were our probable destiny too, and to work in them successfully we would need practice in keeping our neckties tightly knotted and our impulses well damped down. The neckties were subject to visual check, but the impulses proved more difficult to control. Much of the time we gave the necessary lip-service to the idea of appropriate behavior and then did whatever we wanted. The result was a bizarre compound of decorum and chaos—empty decorum, form without content. The school trundled in a septuagenarian named Leyden to teach us some beginning Latin, the archetypal language of order and tradition. Nearly deaf and nearly blind, he frustrated the boys who tried to create various noisy distractions in the corners of the room, for he was sealed off in his dreamy Victorian twilight and virtually undistractible. A favorite ploy of the miscreants was to lift the loose ring around one of the steam pipes all the way to the ceiling and send it spinning and rattling back to the floor, but Leyden just sat there like a bust of Cicero. From time to time he emerged from his reverie to lead us in a rousing Episcopal hymn. We were sure, as we smirked our way through the refrain of "When the Roll Is Called Up Yonder, I'll Be There," that his palsied index finger had fallen from the vertical and was pointing straight toward the underworld.

Of all the faculty at Meadowbrook, the one who loomed largest in my imagination (though he had none at all himself) and who represented the emptiest of empty decorum was "Uncle Doug" Crate. Crate was the school's athletic director and a classic subject for pre-adolescent caricaturists, of whom there were many. Our art factory ran full-bore through every class and used up far more notebook paper than we devoted to notes and homework combined. We drew Crate more often than any other teacher, always exaggerating the vast, bald cranium with its ridiculous white fringe and adding luxuriant tufts of hair from nostrils and ears. In these pass-it-on portraits, he was usually pie-eyed with indignation—which was, in fact, his normal state.

Crate graciously permitted the school administration to plug him in as a teacher of whatever academic discipline happened to be going begging in a given year. Since no course mattered to him, any course was possible. He taught Science, English, Social Studies, all with the same robotic lack of engagement. Once, he admonished us that he was alive to our tricks, and that anyone trying to pad a report with a page of X's and O's in the middle would certainly be caught. I inferred from this warning that the standard was low and that although pure nonsense might not get by, almost anything short of it probably would. "Uncle Doug" was not a man of fine discrimination. The only time his mind flickered into something like life was in the "skull sessions" that he held with the baseball team on rainy afternoons when we could not go outside.

"You're on second with two out and there's a ground ball to short," he would say. "Do you go back to the base, or try to move up?" No arithmetical operation, point of syntax, or current event ever excited in him anything like the intensity of interest he showed at these moments, and the importance with which he invested the question transfigured him from a cartoon character into a figure of menace. I was good at school and, thanks to the tutelage of the Smith men, could certainly have corrected Uncle Doug's grammar more often than he could have corrected mine. I was also a maniacal baseball fan with deep team loyalties and an insatiable appetite for statistics. If he had asked me for the name of the only American League regular that Bob Feller failed to strike out during his then-record season of 1946, I could have told him. However, I was an inept player, scared of the ball and unable to coordinate my intelligence with the activities of hands, arms, and legs. Whatever the theoretical answer to the question, I knew that in a game I would probably get it wrong—would dive back to second and fail to score when the ball dribbled between the shortstop's legs or would impetuously break for third and be tagged out on an alert defensive play.

The knowledge that I was a screw-up often muddled my head so that even there at a desk in the dim upstairs classroom with the raindrops tapping on the panes—a setting in which I didn't actually have to *do* anything—I couldn't figure out what would be the right thing to do on the field. And even when I did figure it out, Uncle Doug knew me. He had seen me play and understood the full extent of my ineptitude. No matter what I might say about the advantages of sticking close to second and watching for an opportunity, he could see in his imagination the delighted shortstop slapping the tag on my sorry, flannel-clad ass.

Uncle Doug didn't like me. For a teacher, he was surprisingly suspicious of and hostile toward all hints of intellectual development, regarding them both as indicators of weakness in the realm of practical affairs and as cunning efforts to circumvent his regime of manly discipline. Compared to the handsome young athletes he cherished, I was nothing but an effeminate smartypants. I didn't like him, either. It especially offended me that he wanted me to call him "Uncle Doug." I already had several perfectly good uncles and did not feel for him the mixture of deference, admiration, and good fellowship that I supposed he meant the title to lay claim to.

Despite our mutual antipathy, Crate kept trying to recruit me to attend his summer camp in Maine, Camp Katahdin, even lugging a projector to our apartment one night so that he could show us a film of the good times to be had there. This aggressive marketing may have been advanced for its time, but the fact that the summit of Mt. Katahdin was the first place in the continental United States from which the sunrise could be seen each day did not seem to me a strong selling point. I imagined the camp, which many of my classmates returned to year after year, as the scene of inane traditions, non-stop sports, and unchecked minor bullying—in other words, as Meadowbrook without the perfunctory and conventional pass at academic life, Meadowbrook as Uncle Doug would have wished it to be. Perhaps he felt that only there, in a pure mental vacuum, could he bring about my complete reformation—or perhaps he just had another bunk to fill. My parents, seeing how much I wanted not to go, told him that they could not afford to send me.

They may have been telling something like the truth. Even if I had not telegraphed my own revulsion, Dad, whose idea of a good time was an evening concert at the Society for Ancient Instruments, who was known as "The Professor" to the men he occasionally played pool with in the neighborhood, and who must have felt in equal parts intimidated by and contemptuous of a thundering dullard like Crate, would have instinctively recoiled from delivering his only son into the man's hands. Still, money was also an issue. A year's tuition at Meadowbrook in the mid-50's ran to $480, a stretch for a family with an income that could barely have attained five digits at the time. The four of us were crammed into what had been the staff quarters of a lawyer's extensive country house in Bethayres, where a consideration in the rent was our willingness to keep an eye on the empty seven-eighths of the place all winter, while the lawyer and his family resided on the Main Line. Our apartment contained only two bedrooms, and since my sister and I had reached the point where we could no longer share one, Mom and Dad had relinquished theirs and taken to a Hide-a-Bed in the living room. We ate at a tiny, enamel-topped table in the kitchen, just clear of the swing of refrigerator and oven doors. If I had desperately wanted to go to summer camp, they would have found a way; but private school *and* camp would have seemed like an extravagance.

Why private school at all, then? Even setting aside Crate as the weak link to be found in any chain, Meadowbrook cannot have offered an education very much superior to what I would have received if I had gone on into public middle school. Yes, the classes were smaller and the all-maleness may have promised a more serious aura, a monastic discipline possible only when there were no girls around. But no such eyes-on-the-prize mentality actually existed. Instead, there was an easy-going macho camaraderie, which my classmates appeared to relish and I faked for all I was worth (when I wasn't running for my life to avoid getting wedgied by Ken Hucke during outdoor "play").

The teachers did try, most of them, and they faced long odds, for the mind of a boy on the cusp of adolescence is at best only dimly responsive to intellectual stimulation and almost entirely resistant to order. But their dominant style was a not very stimulating Copy, Memorize, and Recite. History simplified itself into "The Long March of Democracy," all the weary way from Hammurabi's Code to the present, outlined daily on the blackboard to be transcribed into our notebooks. We were not encouraged to ask any questions about this record of progress but were instead tacitly invited to feel smug about it—and also to shudder at the alternative represented by Communism. The Reds were then in the process of crushing the Hungarian revolt and, so Crate told us with unusual gusto, enjoyed inserting a glass rod into the penis of a captured rebel and then breaking it to bits with a hammer.

His own sadism in recounting the story to 12-year-olds with acutely vulnerable penises came close to matching that of the commissars. We also had a twice-weekly class in "Ethics," which, as interpreted by Dr. Walker's protégé Dr. Malone, meant Bible stories. If Monty Python had been around at the time, its actors would have been hard pressed to exaggerate either the bizarre inconsequence of this material or the reverence with which we were supposed to regard it. We cheated shamelessly on Malone's quizzes, handing the questions to our brethren in the next classroom while he stole a butt in the faculty lounge during break or just whispering the answers to each other right under his nose. It was Ur of the Chaldees, wasn't it? Yes, it was.

If I could have gone through similar motions for free in the Abington public system, why private school at the considerable cost of $480 a year? The answer was in part my family's credulous faith in the inherent value of a good education, which must have seemed good in proportion to what you had to pay out; in part its ingrained *snobisme*, a resolution never to become common as pigs' tracks even if Gaga's way of putting the point seemed a little over the top; and in part its wish to plan pragmatically for a better future. This last, come to think of it, also seems credulous. Granddaddy was the only male in the two prior generations of the family to graduate from college, let alone earn advanced degrees, and what good had all that learning done him, still desperately hoping for a breakthrough as he entered his sixties and then dying in the traces, his marriage a ruin and his carpet machine defunct? What reason was there to believe that educating me would propel the next generation from a Hide-a-Bed to its rightful four-poster? Could a well-knotted tie and a reflexive "sir" pasted over whatever disrespect I might feel at a given moment really make the difference?

Nevertheless, with Terry in the Army and my sister laboring along under the disqualification of being female in a patriarchy that might be sniped at but still held the reins, educating me was the plan. Whether or not Meadowbrook taught better than its public counterpart, it belonged to a system that moved you along to a different place—it was a feeder school. As such, it provided one and only one significant preparation for the schools it fed: the simple fact that you had paid your $480 and been to Meadowbrook. What you bought was a spot on a moving belt that would carry you to the next stage in your assembly without your having to think too much about it. If decorum is a set of conventional moves that make individual choice and volition unnecessary, then it transcends immediate situations and channels the whole progress of a life.

The adage that whom you know is more important than what you know doesn't get the feeder-school arrangement quite right: the key point was whom your school's placement officer knew. Meadowbrook's placement officer knew people in the great private high schools of Philadelphia—Chestnut Hill Academy, Germantown Friends, and, above all, the William Penn Charter School. Even as we invented vulgar parodies of Penn Charter's football cheer, we were in awe of its austere reputation and recognized it as our future. Most of my classmates did go there, but Uncle Carleton had a farther-reaching idea for me. Still in the heyday of his Andover nostalgia, he proposed sending me to boarding school at his (Martha's) expense. His enthusiasm and money were a more powerful conveyor belt. I had no opinion on the matter until I found myself, one September afternoon in 1957, standing outside a huge, ramshackle freshman dormitory and fighting back tears as my parents' car pulled out of the driveway for the long trip south.

Now it is another afternoon, 50-some years later, and I—a grown man, an experienced teacher—am almost ready to weep tears of frustration at the inability of my freshman Exposition class to get centered and get with the program. The process of digesting a starchy cafeteria lunch has produced an intellectual torpor that expresses itself in jittery, spastic physical activity. Even empty decorum would be welcome here: perhaps it would provide a breathing space and some content could eventually be teased out of it. But no, we are at the darkest moment of the retreat from Moscow. Fortunately, I can depend on Meaghan, who I am convinced would still be marching smartly, with bayonet fixed and belt-buckle polished, through greater chaos than this, if such were possible. But even Meaghan's remarkable focus, discipline, and good will—she sits there straight-backed, maintaining steady, hopeful eye-contact with me, notebook open, pencils (even *colored* pencils for underlining) at the ready—can't stand up to the rampant disorder around her.

No two attentions in the room are aimed at the same place. Allen is ogling his lacrosse stick, which he loves more than anything and which he has with the greatest reluctance propped in the corner only because I insisted that he not cuddle it at the table. Charlie, a *Star Wars* aficionado, is daydreaming about light-sabers, which serve a similar adolescent male symbolic function for him and which, being fantasies, he can bring to his seat unobserved: I know they're there, but I can't call him on them. Nat, who often functions as Charlie's sidekick, is today consumed with attempting to make himself so small that I won't notice him, while Tyrone, who would happily swell up to hog all my attention all the time, is rapping out a stream of clever remarks so far off topic that I surely must respond to them. Larry, whose ambition outruns his productivity, is grumbling pre-emptively about the B he expects to get on the paper I'll hand back at the end of class. For some reason he always thinks he has earned an A.

What would the Best Practice be? Would even a rooster jump be enough to pull these pinwheeling consciousnesses toward a common point? I'm afraid I'd break an ankle, so I settle for some ad hoc vocabulary work instead. "Tyrone," I say, "do you know what *drivel* means?" He has the attention he has been angling for, and he is about to learn a new word, one with potent application to himself. Next, we'll try the squirming Allen on *sitzfleisch*, German for buttocks and, by extension, for the ability to sit still. Charlie will get *reverie,* Nat *feckless,* and Larry *hubris.* Meaghan, god bless her, will get *indomitable,* which she will record in her notebook, probably in purple marker. I shelve the planned lesson, hoping to take it up again tomorrow. Gradually the class livens to the realization that I am coming after them in their private spaces. No observer would be likely to mistake the result for a parade-ground review, but perhaps it is a Good Enough Practice for a difficult afternoon.

# Chapter 3

— ◆◆◆ —

# RIGOR

*ANDOVER, MASSACHUSETTS, 1957. The rough twist of the rope pricks my hands as I pull myself up the cargo net. It is not a difficult ascent, even for someone who finds most of the events of this freshman phys ed course next to impossible. The program calls for us to perform various feats involving bars, weights, mats, vaulting horses, medicine balls. Each feat earns a certain number of points, depending on how hard it is. The young teachers who are pressed into service to monitor activity at a half-dozen stations function also as scorekeepers. No actual teaching takes place. No one says, "If you grip the bar this way with your feet, you will get more leverage" or "Use these exercises to build up your shoulder muscles and you'll find that easier." The system simply sorts you out by what you can and can't do. I have little strength, little coordination, little flexibility, and very few points.*

*The cargo net hangs from a beam at one end of the "Old" Gym, a dim place of brick and dark wood wainscots with the aura of 1900 about it. My grandfather's gym, the kind of building on whose steps you'd expect to find neat rows of young men sitting in letter sweaters with their hair parted in the middle and a fat, old-fashioned football with a painted-on score*

(Andover 20, Exeter 16) on the captain's lap. The air inside compounds sweat, fear, varnish, and testosterone into a pervasive fug many decades in the making.

The main function of a cargo net in this pre-containerized era is to swing heavy bundles and bales of stuff out of the hold of a ship and onto a dock. Secondarily, if hung at the vertical, as this one is, it provides a way for men to scramble up and down the ship's side when no gangway is available. The net might have been designed for climbing and clinging, with fresh hand- and footholds every eight inches or so. Only 13 years earlier, soldiers were swarming down cargo nets into their landing craft for the Normandy invasion.

I can get three points for climbing the cargo net and climbing back down the other side. Three points would be a good day's work for me. However, I can score an extra two points and make it a bonanza if, instead of just swiveling my legs and butt across sideways, like some timid, undignified crab, I double over the beam at the top, grasp the rope on the far side, and flip myself into a dangling position, facing outward, before I descend. Why would I want to do this? I don't stop to ask the question. There is no failing grade in phys ed class and no reward for ringing up any particular score. The points are ends in themselves, perfectly sterile ones, pointless as Grant Swartley's algebra, and the feat will never be repeated for either pleasure or profit.

But whatever my physical limits, I have a modicum of heedless courage, if courage is defined as willingness to do something that you are manifestly unprepared to do and may not survive attempting. Perhaps testosterone simply dominates the atmosphere at that altitude, 20 feet above the gym floor. At any rate, I find myself at the top, I bend over the beam, I reach for the rope, I commence my roll.

And then, of course, I am, momentarily, airborne and then I am struggling to my feet on the mat at the bottom of the net and proclaiming, "Jesus Christ, I broke my arm." I feel I have earned the right to blaspheme, and none of the young teachers chastises me for it or, for that matter, seems inclined to look too closely at my right forearm, which is bowed into the shape *of a banana. Later, it will develop that I have also broken my left wrist, though not so spectacularly. I have been at Andover for less than a month.*

All schools that aspire to be more than holding tanks serve a dual function. On the one hand, they must impose the patterns and purposes of society on wild creatures whose natural drift is toward anarchy, and to do this they must apply the system of coercion politely known as "rigor." Schools set limits, demand obedience, channel energy toward commonly sanctioned ends. They are inflexible, authoritarian, and punitive. This may be thought of as their militaristic function, and though it appears at the purest in military schools, every school accepts it to some degree as a necessary part of its mission and every student sees in it one face of the institution he attends. To go to school is to confront the unwelcome fact that you are one of many, that no one else will ever love you as your parents do, that you may, if things go badly, flunk out or be busted and dismissed.

On the other hand, schools serve a therapeutic function. They coax the individual toward his own fulfillment. They encourage questioning and experimentation. They smile at the vicissitudes of the young, offer second chances, want to talk it all over, would rather negotiate than decree. If they can't deal out parental love, they are nevertheless *in loco parentis*, and this removed stance may even prove more nurturing than the cramped intimacy of life with mom and dad. To go to school—especially to go *away* to school—is to discover a world of interesting people who are there for the express purpose of helping you establish and refine your emergent identity, of helping you find out who you are.

The history of boarding schools in the past half-century has been of unsteady but inexorable evolution from the quasi-military to the quasi-therapeutic mode. Andover in 1957, though positively mellow in comparison with some of its peer schools, was still a hard place, unapologetically so. The week I plummeted from the cargo net was the same week the Russians sent Sputnik I into orbit. Its tiny sphere could be seen winking in the night sky, reminding us that we were matched with a cruel and powerful enemy, a breaker of glass rods in the penises of the defeated, and that we would need to toughen ourselves and submit to remorseless discipline in order to prevail. My slightly earlier contemporary Holden Caulfield, in flight from the school that has expelled him, insists with a curious pride that "They give guys the ax quite frequently at Pencey." At this moment he is neither a miserable wretch boasting about how much company he has nor a rebel slamming the system. Rather, he accepts without second thought the basic tenet of 1950's education: that the ax is the guarantor of a school's place in the world of schools and that a regime of selective decapitation is also an effective strategy *pour encourager les autres*.

Andover's top administrators seemed benign enough. Colonel John Mason Kemper, the headmaster, was a West Point man and career officer, tall, straight, and impressively graying, but he projected kindness rather than severity—projected it, to the delight of the school's public relations arm, even from the cover of *Time* magazine a few months before I arrived; G. Grenville Benedict, the Dean of Students, stuck his hands in his pockets and hit just the right arch, amusing note as he discoursed to us from the stage of the big assembly hall like a friendly sheepdog chivvying strays and stragglers into line. We were not to carve new footpaths into all those acres of closely-cropped lawn by following the hypotenuse when the two flagstone legs of the triangle would get us there just as well. We were not to cross, in a cavalier fashion that would alarm motorists speeding toward the racetrack a few miles north, the major highway that bisected the campus. We were not, under any circumstances, to launch bottle rockets from dormitory windows.

Beneath the top tier was an echelon of authorities who did not practice such a gentle massaging of behavior. Perhaps they didn't believe in it, regarded it as a weakness. Perhaps, thinking a little more deeply, they considered it a mode of control possible only because of their own less conspicuous bare-knuckled efforts. The boys in the back room and their assistant bookkeepers tracked the tiniest transgressions and applied the most elaborate system of penalties. If you studied in the library at night, you punched out on a time-clock and then had seven minutes to get back and check in at your dorm, presenting the card as evidence that you had not taken any unauthorized detours. If you dawdled between breakfast and chapel, the tolling bells accelerated to a crescendo and the massive doors swung shut ahead of you; spotters in the balcony zeroed in on the empty seat, consulted their charts, and assigned you a cut. Enough of those and you were "posted"—grounded, though how you could be any more effectively grounded than you already were by the routine of school life is hard to say.

When the transgressions became more serious, the boys in the back room never hesitated to reach for and wield the ax. Two of my classmates lifted some finery (lime green britches? blue belts encircled by spouting whales?) from the preppy clothes store downtown; they were gone the next day. Others got roaring drunk in the shadows of the nearby bird sanctuary, failed to sober up enough to pass muster when they returned, and suffered the same fate. Many, many others simply couldn't keep pace with the academic work; they disappeared more quietly over the summer, or, in extreme, Caulfieldesque cases, over a Christmas or spring break. The discipline system, both social and academic, ground with all the subtlety and compassion of a two-ton millstone, and its insistent pressure came to seem like a natural force, an inevitable condition of school life, rather than a conscious set of choices by the adults in charge.

Once a millstone is in place, it becomes difficult to dislodge. Even fifteen years later, even after the 60's and everything that they entailed, the same remorseless grinding. Those whose schoolwork fell below standards found themselves slotted into one of several categories that took the place of actual attempts to help with their problems. One evening in 1973 the faculty, I among them now, took up the case of a student who was floundering badly. The Dean read off his grades—pathetic. Then someone pointed out that the boy had a severe eye problem, that he was all but going blind. The slightest of pauses ensued. Then we went ahead and voted him on General Warning, the last pigeonhole before expulsion. It seemed like the rigorous thing to do.

In 1957, the sight of a spindly 13-year-old freshman with casts on both arms was enough to engage Andover's gentler side, especially when my course of treatment did not go smoothly. After a week or so, the fractured radius and ulna of my right arm proved so unstable that I had to spend a few days at Mass General having the bones reset and a vanadium plate put in to keep them aligned. I lived at the school infirmary for a month, watched the transit of Sputnik from the conservatory windows at the end of the hall. Mrs. Kemper visited with homemade cookies. The nurses teased and babied me, especially the tall, cute, and feisty Miss Jordan, whose attentions I doted on. Miss Jordan was double-jointed in both elbows and could bend her arms in a way that made them look grotesquely broken, like mine.

My right cast was to stay in place till Christmas, and teachers made allowances for the fact that I could not write. When the weather turned cold and my arms wouldn't fit through the sleeves of a coat, someone arranged for me to have a football cape, a heavy wool garment that the varsity players wore to stay warm on the bench. One rainy Saturday at a game, a student manager assumed that I had stolen it and began to strip it off me, but then he saw those magic casts and buttoned me right back up again. Another time, though the casts dangled under her nose, a vigilant librarian moved in reflexively to kick me out of her building for not wearing the required sports jacket and relented only with the greatest reluctance, as if breaking the arms had been a cunning bit of sophistry to justify breaking the rules. Mostly, though, my plight made others feel tender toward me. It was so palpable that it reduced the stigma the community usually imposed on tender feelings. I even became a minor celebrity.

One of my classmates, Ted Thompson, recently wrote in to our email conference to express the anger he still felt toward the school, which he remembered bitterly as frigid and unforgiving. A powerful, ambitious athlete, he had suffered particularly from coaches who thought of him merely as an asset for victory and relegated him to non-person status when injuries knocked him out of the lineup. When one of them at last spoke kindly to him, a couple of years into his Andover career, he was so inured to the deep-freeze treatment that he experienced the overture as weird and could no longer find in himself the warmth to respond to it.

Swaddled in my cloak of immunity and relieved for the time being of all contact with the formidable athletic machine, I nevertheless did witness treatment that by today's standards seems both stunningly severe and inexcusably self-indulgent. Often it took the straightforward form of a savage scolding. A math teacher, Jack McClement, was famous for his tirades, which could occur at any place and time. Detecting some slight disruption in the auditorium at the Saturday night movie, he threw on the lights, leapt to the stage, bawled us out, and sent all 600 of us back to our dorms. Since the misbehavior had been invisible to almost everyone, we learned no lesson but were left only with the impression of a scrawny, red-faced madman in bottle-bottom glasses, stamping his foot and screeching like an enraged Rumpelstiltskin. McClement also had a habit of erupting from the bushes like a G-man to collar and berate minor miscreants.

My Latin teacher, John Colby, looked to be about the same age as Meadowbrook's Leyden, but whereas Leyden had been happy enough just to survive, Colby meant business. On his watch, there would be no foolery with the heating system. Colby had written the book on Latin 1—his name was right there on the title page—and he drove home its precepts with glacial force. The nature of his relationship with us was clear from the geography of the classroom in Andover's Classics building, which made the "Old" Gym where I came to grief look as if it had been designed by Mies van der Rohe. In the gloomy, echoing chamber lined with plaster statuary and sepia shots of the Forum and the Coliseum in heavy brown frames, Colby looked down at us from a massive desk mounted on a foot-high podium, while we looked up at him from rows of benches bolted to the floor. Lest there be any doubt that freshman boys were as worms before the eternal truth of the First Declension (and other declensions to come), he emphasized the point with unsparing humiliation. The ax waiting in the background might be a keen-edged mercy in comparison with the bludgeoning to be endured beforehand. When he returned a test, Colby would not simply hand you your paper but instead would post on the blackboard the grades of everyone in the class and offer scathing commentary on them. "Now Andy Blake, who has had Latin before, got a 55 on this test—55 percent, Andy. That's a disgrace." And so on, itemizing each inaccurate ending and bone-headed mistranslation. Inspired by this diatribe and relieved that I had scored somewhat higher than the wretched Blake, I did not think the moment was right to remind Colby that I, too, had "had" Latin before.

Today, Blake would be on his cell to his parents within five minutes of the end of class and the phone on the Dean's desk would be ringing five minutes after that. The Dean would cluck sympathetically, temporize, assure the Blakes that this sort of thing was an unfortunate anomaly. Then he would ask Colby to drop by and would lay out the parameters of the new dispensation. Posting grades on the blackboard violates students' privacy. Singling out a boy for public criticism destroys his self-esteem. And what about young John's 55—mightn't he fairly have been given a few more points on the Latin-to-English section? Unspoken in the background of the conversation would be the awareness that parents may become litigious on almost any pretext and that even if they do not go to law, the prop-wash of their hovering can make it a windy day for everyone in the vicinity. The contemporary Colby would feel resentful and old and would calculate anew whether he had enough in the bank to support retirement. But of course there could not be a contemporary Colby.

In 1957, teachers had enormous space to develop and practice their tyrannies. Supervision was scant and communication with home was slow. A tale of injustice lost color and freshness when recounted a week later at the dorm pay phone while others waited for their turn. And, above all, tyranny was just a part of the landscape, the alkali flats that you knew you had to cross in order to get wherever your education was taking you. Some parents may have been inclined to wade in on their children's behalf, but most would have resisted the impulse. They would have felt that the school knew its business, that discipline was necessary for growing up, even that they were paying the school precisely to apply its rigors on their behalf. Most of my classmates seemed to accept these premises too. I would certainly have dissolved in tears if Colby had come after me that way, but Blake just sat there and took it stoically, perhaps pinkening a bit in the cheeks.

The wonder may be that most Andover teachers were as mild as they were. Their egos must have swelled with the knowledge that they were at the top of their profession, that they taught in what *Time* magazine had anointed as the country's leading school. Yet the profession that they were at the top of was a poor one, miserably underpaid. They probably earned $6000 a year. Their often squalid housing had to be shared at close quarters with herds of noisy, smelly, and devious adolescents. They were saddled with endless preparations and supervisory duties. Scanning for empty seats from a chapel balcony, keeping the lid on a dark auditorium at a movie you had no interest in seeing, making the rounds night after night to confirm that your charges had not slipped out to town, finally getting down to your stacks of papers and your lesson plans while your wife understandably sulked and your own children whined for a shred of your attention—these conditions of life eroded the pride of place, made teachers feel less like revered elders and more like sheriff's deputies or narcs. Whipsawed between high and low conceptions of themselves, they naturally were jealous of their prerogatives and all too ready to blow.

If not the very center of the school's power, the athletic machine that ground up Ted Thompson was a vast, independent satrapy with designs on the throne. Its clout arose partly from the extent of its real estate—old gym, new gym, pool, rink, field house, and fields that stretched over the prime terrain at the crest of Andover hill to an expanse known as Outer Siberia where the scrubs broke their daily sweat—all tended by platoons of groundsmen and fleets of expensive equipment for mowing, fertilizing, aerating, rolling, and lining. A zamboni, brand new at the time and miraculous to watch, smoothed the way for the hockey team between periods. Modified golf carts brought in the injured from the far reaches of the empire so that trainers could patch them up and return them to the fray. To take a battering and get right back at it was the prevailing manly ethos, a lesson learned in preparation for the no-quarter world of American enterprise as well as for the struggle against Communism. Yes, we needed to refine our intelligence, but no intelligence would serve us unless we were also tough. Toughening us was the business of sports and the reason, beyond mere territorial dominion, that the athletic complex enjoyed the stature that it did. Few of us would ever have thought to question this pre-eminence, for to boys the physical is almost always more real, more urgent, and more fun than the cerebral.

Even I, the Cerebral Kid, a puny excuse for an athlete and an instant, egregious victim of the complex, found the tug of sports irresistible and regarded *getting back on the horse* as an imperative for restoring self-respect. In the spring, when the plate had been removed from my arm, I rejoined the phys ed program for its swimming and drownproofing segment. We kicked furiously to keep a pair of five-pound weights from driving us to the bottom of the diving pool and learned to float in the approved position that, though corpse-like, had kept men from torpedoed troopships alive for many hours in the waters of the Pacific. On the last day, with nothing but a few extra points to gain by it, I held my breath long enough to swim 50 yards—two full laps of the pool—underwater, bursting to the surface with empty lungs and an elated sense of accomplishment. The scorekeepers cited me in a report sent home. I was a poster child for their program, a boy who had literally shattered himself and returned to action, proof that rigor worked. I did not object to playing the part.

Phys ed, for freshmen only, was just a supplement to the daily exertions at the core of the athletic program. That every student would break a sweat every day reigned as the ultimate unalterable law in a school full of unalterable laws. Between 2:00 and 4:00 each afternoon, we fanned out over that huge acreage of fields and courts, checked in with our teams, played. The system was a finely tuned hierarchy. Varsity teams trained with knowledgeable coaches, dressed in sharp, expensive uniforms, and ran on fields that might have been laid out and ruled by Euclid himself. Several strata of JV teams developed those who could aspire to varsity in another year but weren't quite there yet; they wore varsity cast-offs, and their fields might have an odd angle, a bare spot, a bump or two. Finally—athletics for all!—came the "club" teams, which were not clubs in the normal sense but randomly-assigned units for the uncoordinated, the inexperienced, and the indifferent. Their coaches were conscripts like themselves, non-athletes in their own school days, there to take attendance, herd, and organize but rarely competent to teach the first thing about the game being played. The players' only uniforms were tee-shirts color-coded to the "clubs" they supposedly belonged to, which had been named in the already long-gone era when Classics were a universal frame of reference: Romans, Saxons, Greeks, and Gauls. The Siberian fields where the action took place were hillocky, barren, and hard, with the occasional rock outcrop where trampling feet had worn the poor soil away. Every square inch was needed to accommodate the games. In the most popular sports, like soccer and baseball, there were even two levels of club teams, "A" club and "B" club.

From the first, even before I broke my arms, it was clear that I would be a bottom feeder in this enormous fishery, a B-clubber's B-clubber. I had played soccer at Meadowbrook but had learned nothing about it there, and Bill Logan was not about to instruct me. A tall, wan, fragile

Latin teacher without either physical presence or the slightest aptitude for engaging the spirits of adolescent boys, he made it clear that he regarded his coaching as an unfortunate condition of employment. He scratched our names off the list and stood around dutifully to monitor the required sweat. We played as best we could. Even on B club, almost everyone was better than I was. Then I did break my arms and the Romans had to make do without me for most of the fall and winter.

The ladder of athletic authority rose from Bill Logan on the lowest rung to Ted Harrison at the top. Harrison had come out of a nearby mill town to attend Andover in the 30's and had been a legendary three-sport athlete. Part of the legend was a titanic home run that he had struck against Exeter, a blast that one-hopped the wall of the field house a good 450 feet from home plate. A strong student, too, he had gone on to Yale, done a post-grad year at one of the English universities, and then served as an officer in Europe during the war.

Pity the German patrol that ran into Harrison on the fields of France. Unlike Logan and like our most noteworthy military man, Headmaster Kemper, Harrison had physical presence to burn. But the resemblance ended there. Kemper's presence was patrician—lean, handsome, decorous, surprisingly gentle. Harrison came on like the mill-town roughneck he had been, exuding a whiff of class animus even as he exulted in his position in the new class. He wore his hair in a fierce flattop that made his skull look like a fist. His nose appeared to have been flattened in some kind of street brawl. His speech was a rubble of stony consonants; despite the sojourn at Oxford, he still said *dis*, *dat*, *dese*, and *dose*.

Naturally, I was afraid of Harrison, but I was also fascinated by him. Whatever social cliffs he had had to scale, he now radiated an unshakeable self-assurance about his place in the world and his ability to dominate his chosen realms. Even as a boy I knew that such self-assurance had to contain a measure of self-delusion and that such dominance depended on crushing some of the color and subtlety out of what you dominated. But still. I had never met anyone with Harrison's unequivocal force. He was Crate with a brain but also Crate without the smarmy pretenses. No way was Ted Harrison, who had hit the field house on one bounce, who had smelled the smoke of burning armor and heard the cries of wounded men, who was director of athletics for a school of 800, about to ask any of us to call him "Uncle Ted."

When I was assigned to Harrison's American history class in my senior year, I saw his limits. He had mastered the facts but only the facts. His knowledge lacked allusiveness and connectivity. The method (which was the method of the entire history department) involved our taking a pre-printed outline of topics and filling in the spaces with notes from our nightly reading. Harrison rarely had much to add to what we had scoured from the text, and he was not a talented explainer. One day I asked him how it was possible that in the crash of 1929 the value of the stock market could have disappeared overnight. "Well, I'll tell you, David," he said, scratching his flattop reflectively, "people were papering their walls with those"—*dose*—"worthless stock certificates." It was a vivid image but not an answer to my question.

By this time, however, I was fully in thrall to the athletic machine. It had sucked me into its premises, massaged me until I looked forward to the 2:00-4:00 pm slot as the best part of the day. I was still a clubber, but an A-clubber now—a competent soccer goalie, a swimmer who could gain points for his team, a reliable third baseman and .300 hitter for the Roman nine. And I had worked my way up through the ranks of the weekly newspaper, the *Phillipian*, to become its sports editor. We ran a rigorous ship, my cronies and I, doing everything on our own, without input from our faculty advisor, who did not weigh in until an issue had hit the stands, and even then sparingly. I have never had a better lesson in the educational value of independence and practice. We had learned the trade by working for the editors before us and we kept on learning it, week by week, when we were in charge. Being in charge meant we were responsible for the product, and being responsible motivated us to make it as good as it could be. Today when I see teachers hovering too close, trying too hard to control everything that happens, I think, *Stand back and give those kids some room to own what they do.* We would sooner have died than fail to get our edited copy to the printshop downtown by the deadline, and we relished every inch of what came floating off the old-fashioned letterpress with its little row of gas flames to dry the ink.

We knew about objectivity, too, and respected it. The primary purpose of the sports page was to deliver information, not to serve as a surrogate cheerleader for the Royal Blue. We covered every interscholastic game in a separate article with a lead that included the score and a carefully crafted summary of highlights. (As most teams played two games a week, this was a tall order.) We printed box scores and season statistics. We went out of our way to learn opponents' names. We lavished as much detail on the Andover catastrophes as on the successes. I often stayed up half the night polishing the rough edges off what the reporters brought in. Everything had been typed, double-spaced, on manual typewriters. Sometimes, when the roughness extended beyond the edges, there was no room to jam in the hand-written corrections in a way that the typesetter would be able to comprehend. Then it was easier just to rewrite the whole story and type it anew.

A compensation for all this detail work was my weekly column, "On the Sidelines." My flaming red hair had prompted almost everyone at school to call me Red from the beginning; now I could share a by-line with the greatest sportswriter of the age, Red Smith, whose columns for the New York *Herald* brilliantly bridged locker room and literary salon. I aspired to the like, was always on the lookout for the vein of poetry in my material. Often it emerged from my hand as pretentious bombast, inflated verbiage wildly at odds with content. Still, it looked like poetry to me. I saw sports as drama and myth, populated by heroes who, though they might sit down next to me at lunch, acquired an unearthly glow as soon as they stepped onto a playing field and who performed feats that were to a clubber's awkward striving as blank verse was to an average classified ad. "Moose" Hackett,

Pete Preston, "Beaver" Gibson, Dave Murphy, Steve Kehas, Toby Hay, "Bumstead" Brown. What I wrote about them made up in adulation whatever it lacked in eloquence.

Harrison liked what I wrote. In the spring of my senior year he asked me to take part in a student panel that would make a presentation on Andover athletics to a council of alumni. The hidden agenda—I don't remember how I knew this—was to extort the money for a second hockey rink. Hearing from real students would make the alums feel in touch with the scene in a way that would also make their wallets more accessible. One of us was to speak for the varsity athlete, one for the club athlete, and one for the non-athlete. Of course, realistically speaking, there could be no non-athletes at Andover, and not for another decade or more did anyone dare even to suggest that perhaps—just one season a year?—working on stage crew or serving meals at a homeless shelter in Lawrence might legitimately replace the daily sweat. It was somewhat out of character for Harrison to acknowledge the existence of the non-'s. He must have thought he could score some points for verisimilitude.

The good news in the presentation plan was that I myself could no longer be cast as the non-. I was Mr. Club—in this arrangement, a status point. No one coached us on what to say, but I knew my part. I wittily applied major league lingo to the progress of the Romans' baseball season, won a wave of laughter by quoting an apt line from Housman's "To an Athlete Dying Young," left them with some earnest thoughts about everything that club sports had done for me, sat down to appreciative applause. Harrison didn't get his spare rink (an alum who controlled the till observed that a rink is much like a drink—when you have one, you immediately want another), but I had held up my part of the deal. My talk was printed in the alumni magazine. I had become not just a poster child for freshman phys ed but a mouthpiece for the whole Andover athletic program, and I embraced its iron bosom as though it were my nurse.

# Chapter 4

———∙∞∙———

# HUMANITY

*HARRISON SCHUYLER "SCOTTY" Royce looks a little the worse for wear this morning—though the distinction is not easy to make, because he always looks very much the worse for wear. Probably no more than 40, he nevertheless has the deeply furrowed brow of an older man, and he walks stiffly, bent a few degrees forward over the fastened bottom button of his sport coat, with his squared-off knit tie hanging straight down like a plumb bob. When he talks, gravel seems to be pouring out the back of a dump truck in long, rumbly slides. We know for what passes among schoolboys as a fact that he has a steel plate in his head, a souvenir of the Pacific theater.*

*All these engaging style points hint at a past to be unraveled, and Royce's present has equal appeal: he is one of those teachers who not only can claim to exist outside the borders of their classroom but even possess a hearty appetite for life as it is lived out there, an intriguing* joie de vivre. *He has a beautiful wife, perhaps his own age but seemingly much younger. The afternoon a couple of years earlier when I arrived at school for the first time, in full terror of being abandoned by my parents, Ann Royce's presence among the greeters in the huge, dim freshman dormitory was one of the few things that kept my knees from buckling altogether. Or she distracted me from my anguish by making them buckle in another way. Like the kind of female star I favored in the old movies that I would watch into the early morning hours on summer nights, actresses with names like "Phyllis" and "June," she was kind and sweet yet discreetly perfumed with sexuality—a boy's dream of a grown woman.*

*Scotty and Ann have four children, but the kids don't cramp their entertainment schedule. The night before Christmas break in freshman year, I lay awake after curfew and listened to one of their parties cranking up in the dorm common room downstairs. A display of northern lights fluttered in the sky outside my window, and the streamers seemed to coincide with the waves of music and hilarity rising from below. Everyone was having a very good time.*

*Weekend or school night, the Royces have their fun, and this 8:12 European history class can therefore sometimes be…difficult…for him. Once he did not appear at all and the official word was that some tainted oysters had made him sick; we recognized this for the euphemism it was. Mostly, after a night of it, he gets here—but the furrows are a little deeper, the bend becomes a bit more pronounced, and the gravel slide takes on a rueful overtone. So it does today as he begins expounding on British mercantilism.*

*Royce is a very good teacher. His own history merges with the subject he teaches. That he never says a word about his service, the plate in his head or any of it, merely makes our sense of it more powerful. In addition to the facts and concepts on which he will test us, we acquire from him a philosophy, come to understand that history is a compound of myth, loss, irony, and unintended consequence. He studs his discourse with paradoxical aphorisms—"The men of the far left and the far right are closer together than those on the center aisle"—and leaves us to figure out what they mean. He loves to tell about how the British in Singapore aimed their great guns seaward to repel a naval invasion and the Japanese struck overland through jungle that had been thought impassible.*

*Images and* aperçus *like these will serve us well in a few years, as we try to make sense of the twisted 60's, with their many strange bedfellows and attacks from behind. For now, we simply respond to the drama in front of us—a real person, strung out between history and hangover, his shoulders hunched, his tie dangling, his mind trying to wrestle mercantilism into some language that 16-year-olds can comprehend.*

*I keep two notebooks for history class. One is the official cookbook, the department's outline of topics to be covered, with spaces for us to fill in the details; it's a step up from Meadowbrook's "Long March of Democracy," but only a baby step. The other notebook contains my own grid for recording the abundant and peculiar mannerisms of Royce's speech. In him, the throat-clearing of academic parlance has metastasized into full-blown rococo. For all its sophistication and even wisdom, his talk is a pastiche of prefabricated bits and pieces, and he can scarcely utter a sentence without including one or more of them. Every antithesis emerges as "on the one hand" this and "on the other hand" that; sometimes, if another idea comes crowding in, a third hand magically materializes. Metaphors are signaled by "if you will," an almost plaintive request for our collusion, and are sometimes accompanied by the first finger quotes I have ever seen. Latin appears both in abbreviation ("i.e.," "e.g.") and in full phrases ("per se," "quid pro quo"). Most astonishingly, he appears to think that "the fact remains" is some kind of compound noun that can form the subject of a sentence and must be followed by a verb: it always comes out as "the fact remains is," or, fastidiously, "the fact remained was."*

*My grid provides space for a running tally of the standards and an additional area below for unusual and peachy expressions. I have perfected my ability to get the drift of even such a boring topic as mercantilism and still keep accurate score. Tonight I'll compare totals with my friend in Royce's afternoon section and we'll update the graphs we maintain.*

*"The fact remains is that in essence what it amounted to, however..." Scotty is saying. Despite a headachy squint, he is warming to his task. My pencil flies over the page. I am an assiduous note-taker.*

Later on, I would write, take all the parts in, and record a radio play about Scotty in which he appears as Scott Harris Rice, "the top U. S. State Department trouble-shooter in the Far East." A Red cell is stirring up the dock workers on some dimly-conceived Asian waterfront, and Rice moves in to squash it, growling things like "Where are they, Chiang—i.e., the Communist leaders?" and "You asked for it; ipso facto, you get it." The music, grandly though anomalously, is my dad's 78 rpm of Wagner's *Meistersinger* overture. The title of the play is "The Suave American," "suave" being, in the lexicon I shared with my classmates, the ultimate accolade.

Much later still, after I had been a teacher myself for a long time, I gradually came to realize one of the core truths of our profession: that we can never know what is actually being learned and that it is probably something quite different from what we think we are teaching. At best, perhaps, we teach some of what we mean and much else that we are and will remain completely unaware of. Like history, teaching is a realm of unintended consequence. Twenty years out, no one who has not himself become a math teacher remembers the Quadratic Formula—that much is a cliché. Yet students may, even as they forget the content, adopt the shape of the container, for better or for worse, retaining our meanness, our mannerisms, our pomposity, our compassion, our healing humor, while facts and theorems go skittering into oblivion.

Royce, to whom chance assigned me for two years, was one of those rare teachers who fuse all their messages, conscious and unconscious, into a single irresistible and strongly personal communiqué—who step forward from the flat scrim of school routine and reveal their messy, three-dimensional humanity. Delighted and distracted as I was by the dear quirks of language, I never lost sight of the complex man who uttered them—blown up, patched together, uxorious, paternal, gruff, drunk, smart, and indisputably suave. I recognized something heroic in the labor with which he ginned up his intelligence for us every day and something courtly in the way he addressed us—Mr. Wright, Mr.

Cross, Mr. Smith. And I learned, along with much else about history, that it is to be lived in as well as studied.

The corner of history that I lived in at Andover between 1957 and 1961 was, to be sure, an enclave, as aloof as it could manage to be from the forces that were beginning to churn America and would soon be blowing the top off. I am often annoyed by people's condescending assumption that schools are not part of the "Real World," but there is no denying that we inhabited, in many respects, a dreamland. Its tightly-defined borders no doubt helped to keep us focused on our studies but also set off a cloistered space that left our own nascent humanity insufficiently challenged and stimulated. For Sunday dinner in Commons, we ate the all-white meal—turkey, mashed potatoes, cauliflower, vanilla ice cream with butterscotch sauce, milk—an emblem of our monochrome existence. My class of 220 had one African-American in it, a population density so rarefied that he simply disappeared into the crowd. Tall, affable, and conspicuously dark-skinned, Henry Jones was subsumed at once by the confraternity of jocks, his identity registered as "athlete" rather than as "black." Anyone at school, man or boy, including me, would have said that the "acceptance" of Henry Jones exemplified Andover and America at their best, expressed the democratic principle in its ultimate form. Despite the Montgomery bus boycott, despite Little Rock, no one dwelled on the possibility that enormous injustices were yet to be addressed or that a key part of both white boys' and black boys' education might be to confront boys of other colors and cultures on a more or less equal basis.

On the question of going to school with girls, opinion was more divided. To me, however, the monastic life seemed just fine. Once I got the hang of male camaraderie, it became, in fact, altogether too comfortable. The longer I spent in the cloister, the more girls evolved into idealized creatures of the imagination—delicious to dream on, paralyzing to meet. I would pay heavily, in college and later on, for this lack of experience, would have to make all my early-teen mistakes simultaneously with my late ones and at an age that doubled their inherent misery. But at the time, what I didn't know was just one fewer thing to think about.

I had many friends who stood ready to teach me about girls and other extra-curricular topics. It was no surprise, when I arrived at Andover, that most of my classmates were better athletes than I was, but to discover that many of them were also smarter was unnerving. Smart—at least until I could re-tool as Mr. Club—was where my identity was staked. Though my grandfather and father had insisted on demonstrating that I did not know every word in the world, they had spurred me to make up the deficit as rapidly as possible, and I had always known more words than my schoolmates. At Meadowbrook, my one serious intellectual competitor was Bobby Steer. Bobby and I reached, early on, a *rapprochement*—a tacit agreement that we were equally smart, with a slight edge to him in science and to me in literary arts. Now I was suddenly surrounded by boys who not only could talk rings around me but had also thought about things that I had never thought about before—which was almost everything, as no one had ever really asked me to think. One of these boys was John Ewell, the son of a Yale physician. I roomed with or near John for my last three years; his endearingly gentle, almost goofy persona concealed a target-rifle mind that outshot me in every course we took together. Another was Bill Drayton, who won a library prize for his collection of books on Asia and started a student Asia Society; Bill went on to a creative career in international development and philanthropy. The schools of the 50's would have hesitated to admit that we learn at least as much from our contemporaries as from our elders, but we do—and I thank these two, among many others, for what they taught me.

I lagged even farther behind on the scale of worldliness. In fact, I scored pretty close to zero, a babe in the woods. Andover admitted many boys from New York and its upper-crusty suburbs—Rye, Greenwich, Darien. These guys were professors of worldliness, had their doctorates in it before they even entered high school. They made

Meadowbrook's Gates and Dunham, who had seemed quite knowing at the time, look like country bumpkins. Their knowledge extended from such grand themes as sex, liquor, and trends in Manhattan night life to minutiae like the proper way of putting your hands in your pockets when wearing a sport jacket or of binding your split loafers together with adhesive tape to demonstrate insouciance. Converging on Andover from their well-oiled feeder schools, they were too successful in setting the tone of the place.

Of a somewhat different cast but also far advanced in their studies were Rich Walters and Roy Burton, bad actors who didn't last beyond freshman year but made a big splash while they were with us. Rich and Roy, who had serendipitously been assigned as roommates, rang up record-setting numbers of the "Deficiency Reports" awarded by our dormmasters for minor infractions and barely seemed to notice the ensuing work hours. Their minds were set on higher things. Once, they reported back to us on a double date they had arranged with a couple of girls from town. The evening had ended with Rich and Roy squirting water over one girl's private parts. "And she *liked* it," Rich said, "— the douchy broad." Their exploit struck me as sensational enough, and it raised some interesting questions, such as what "douchy" meant and why Rich evidently looked down on the girl for enjoying something he himself had done to her. But I was not tempted to try it myself.

More titillating were the experiences narrated by another of my roommates, Rick Rhoads. Energetic, irreverent, and opinionated, Rick initially made friends with me by whipping me repeatedly at chess. I saw in him not only a fierce intelligence but also a probable ally against the dominion of the WASP sophisticates. Though he too came from New York, he was an atheist, a Jew, a political radical, and a public school product, the son of a teacher and summer camp director. Rick did scorn the Darien boys but was as interested in sex as they were. I at first dismissed his talk on this subject as fanciful but gradually came to hear a ring of authenticity in it. Oh, those nights with the female campers from Great Neck! Rick once wrote a short story that he had certainly taken from life. It contained lines like "We were both 16, and fully sexually equipped" and "Her nipples were hard as diamonds." This sort of thing seemed more like it than Rich and Roy's adventures with water pistols. Still, I was content with the voyeur's position. A couple of hundred girls resided just down the hill, at Abbott Academy, and there were ways of evading the surveillance system that protected them from us. I preferred to regard it as impenetrable.

Whatever we learned from one another in late-night bull sessions or sitting around the lunch table and whatever the sports juggernaut might demand of us, our formal lessons were the core of our lives. We loved them or hated them, embraced them or resisted them, but we had to take them seriously or quit. Andover's unshakeable institutional self-regard, its crushing glacial force, carried away all before it in a surge of education by coercion. We are right to question the arrogance of this approach today and to congratulate ourselves for living in a daintier time, one in which coaxing and co-optation have supplanted force as the primary tools in the kit. The work is meaningless unless you choose to do it, we say; and the answers are empty unless the questions are your own. So. But Andover did make us believe in the absolute centrality of intellectual life, and that is no small accomplishment for any school.

In the brief interval before school actually began in my freshman year, I saw posted here and there a broadsheet covered with fine print and headed "Schedule of Recitations." At first I wondered what this could mean. Were we going to be asked to recite something, and if so, what? Or perhaps something would be recited to us? Eventually it dawned on me that "recitations" were classes and the fine print on the broadsheet was the key to the card I had been given with my own schedule on it.

When I got to my classes, I found that something like recitation was in fact the dominant style. Colby's Latin classroom, though unusually grim, was not the only one in which neat rows of student desks faced the teacher at the front. This arrangement was the norm, and it implied the primacy of the teacher, his position as a fount of knowledge and authority. Teachers ordinarily did not lecture and would probably have said that student participation was an essential part of their method. We did participate—by answering when called on and reciting what we had gleaned from our studies the night before. The process may have had its virtues, but scintillation was not often one of them. My math teacher, Douglas Durham, simply plodded through the previous evening's problem set, asking one of us for the answer to each problem and correcting the mistakes. Other teachers probed a little harder for understanding, posed followup questions, and pushed us to get ideas into our own words. But always "Did you do your homework?" was the strong subtext; and rarely were we asked to react as people rather than as receptacles for content.

Most teachers were neither as tyrannical as Colby nor as flamboyantly fascinating as Royce. A few lacked convincing command of their subjects but most were real scholars and seemed to feel that their mission was to make us scholars too. As we grew older, the best of them gradually weaned us from the recitation mode and began asking us to think. Colby himself, when I encountered him a second time as my Virgil teacher in junior year, appeared to have forgiven us for our earlier childish groping and to regard us as actual minds, capable not only of deciphering difficult Latin text but also of appreciating, if only dimly, the high literary culture that produced it. Rocky Dake, who taught Chemistry, yielded to no one in irascibility—harsh though the climate was, I was still shocked when he excoriated one boy as a "stupid ass"—but won real respect by demanding nothing less than total comprehension of the concepts, a grasp that we could demonstrate only by being able to apply them to fresh data. I disappointed him sorely when, after nailing the easy material at the start of the course, I lost my grip on the increasingly complex ideas and subsided into mediocrity. My decline was slow enough to avoid the stupid ass tripwire, but both Dake and I could see that I did not have a scientific bent. At about this time I decided that I would not become an engineer like my father and grandfather but would strike out in a new and more forgiving direction.

The English department was the only department in the school that arranged students in something like a circle. In its domain, the elegant, high-ceilinged Bulfinch Hall, we occupied tablet-arm chairs on the periphery of a classroom or clustered around a massive, oval table in the center. The message of a circle is that all points have equal status; when the points are people, all voices count the same. Since the teacher sat in the circle with us, he implicitly ceded to each of us a share of his preeminence. We were to understand that literary texts had multiple and ambiguous meanings and that even the rawest reader brought a unique perspective to bear on them. Instead of meek vessels to be topped up with information, we would become active participants in a small, egalitarian learning community.

This premise was quite radical for its time and place. Teachers in other departments may well have raised their eyebrows at it, and not every English teacher understood or accepted it or knew how to put it into practice. In fact, what authority to yield and what authority to maintain is the great conundrum of teaching in any but a totalitarian style, and, as I would learn myself, teachers who give it all away find soon enough that they would like some of it back. Once we have decided to be less than absolute monarchs, we must decide minute by minute when to honor the parliamentary principle and when to bring the gavel decisively down.

The men of Andover in the 1950's cannot have been comfortable about sharing any kind of authority with teenagers. They had struggled through the Depression, risked their lives in the military to defeat a bitter enemy, submitted unquestioningly to the most rigid chain of command. They had earned their authority. Were they now to bandy words on an equal basis with kids who didn't even have to shave regularly and who couldn't always tell the difference between a noun and verb? It came hard. For most of them, the circular classroom was probably no more than a gesture, and for some it was a gesture imposed on them rather than freely chosen. They kept right on teaching as though they were on a podium and the students neatly lined up before them, awaiting enlightenment.

My freshman English teacher, Donald Peters, was one of these. He was not so much jealous of his authority as unable to imagine any alternative to it; in fact, he could not imagine much of anything. I likened him to Mr. Pumblechook, a minor character in *Great Expectations*, the novel we read that fall. The name suggested Peters's physical and intellectual ponderousness, and the two did share a red, bulbous nose. In Pumblechook's case, this feature resulted from overindulgence in port and sherry; in Peters's, it must have been a natural circulatory effect. He was, if not a teetotaler, a very sober man. His sobriety stripped him of personality. He flatlined: no bad oysters, no idiosyncratic expressions, no thunderous outbursts of pique. He would have recoiled in prissy horror to hear another teacher call a student a stupid ass. Instead, he treated us with an earnest, detached, and thoroughly boring evenness. The decorum was stifling. In a whole year with Peters, I do not remember a single moment of humor or spontaneity, a single laugh.

Peters had his lesson plan dutifully prepared on notecards, from which he read the questions he chose to ask. His heart did not seem to be in these questions. He was the kind of teacher I later learned to recognize as an administrator-in-waiting, one who pays his dues in the classroom so that he can move up as quickly as possible to positions of greater authority in the school hierarchy. A decade or so along, he did in fact become the headmaster of another famous boarding school. In the meantime, he droned at us. The questions were not the only things that emerged with the tinny cadences of one of today's automated telephone trees. He produced the same effect when he read literature aloud, ruthlessly purging Dickens, Hardy, and Shakespeare of their lyricism and emotional color.

I cheated one day in Peters's class. He was giving us a quiz on *Pilgrim's Progress*. I had done the reading, more or less, but it bored me silly and I couldn't remember the details. Whom *did* Pilgrim meet after he got through the Slough of Despond? The tablet arm of my friend Jack Williams's chair intruded provocatively on my peripheral vision. With a will of their own, it seemed, my eyes flicked over to his paper. Mr. Worldly Wiseman. I wrote it down—a Worldly Wiseman thing to do—and tackled the remaining questions on my own. Jack and I turned out to be correct. This was my second narrow escape of freshman year. One more quarter rotation in my plunge from the cargo net and I could have been a paraplegic for life. If Peters had caught me plundering my neighbor's paper, the ax would have been a distinct possibility. My fear of punishment was as strong as the next person's, and I didn't like guilt, either. I never cheated again.

Peters droned on at us through winter and into spring. And then— hail to the Law of Unintended Consequence! Or perhaps it was the Law of *Unlikely* Consequence. Perhaps he did intend to inspire us, though I believe it's more likely that he thought in terms of "inculcating the fundamentals of reading and writing" and regarded inspiration as the province of the Religion department (also ill suited to the task—another story). At any rate, no one observing Peters's class could possibly have mistaken his style for inspirational, and yet suddenly I was inspired, I was in love with literature, I couldn't get the language out of my mind.

I had grown up with books, had read early and been praised for it by family and teachers. Throughout my socially awkward childhood, books had been entertainment, escape, and refuge. I read C. S. Forester's Hornblower stories as soon as they appeared in the *Saturday Evening Post* and devoured stacks of Ray Bradbury, Isaac Asimov, and Robert E. Heinlein science-fiction novels, often hiding out in barn lofts or back rooms to enjoy my fix without annoying intrusions of a practical kind. I had a big vocabulary and an ear for sentence structure. But now, in the spring of freshman year, in a class where nothing ever seemed to happen, something different was happening. Yes, I was flatout, over-the-top, madly in love.

The seduction began with *Richard II*, early Shakespeare and my first. I didn't care about or pay the slightest attention to the politics and genealogy, the tension between Divine Right and human incompetence. What I fell in love with was the music. The pentameters ran in my head like a Mozart symphony, brisk, nimble, melodious, or like an opera in which the plot is incomprehensible and the meaning of the words hardly matters. Whole chunks of the play were in riming couplets, which made the sound of it even more delicious. People actually insulted each other in riming couplets, a tasty sweet-and-sour effect punched up still further by archaisms and inversions:

> Once more, the more to aggravate the note,
> With a foul traitor's name stuff I thy throat.

I memorized hundreds of lines without even trying to and began sparring matches in Elizabethan English with my friends. At the end of the year the class spent a few weeks reading poetry from a paperback anthology, a further revelation. Two crows sat down on a dead knight's breastbone and delicately picked out his bright blue eyes? This was an image that even the Peters monotone could not rob of its startling beauty.

And then, as a sophomore, I was assigned to an honors English section taught by Emory Basford, who blew gently on the coals of my infatuation with literature until it gathered into a lifelong flame and who, more than any other, led me with his humane example to decide that I would be a teacher.

How Emory did this is still not entirely clear to me, and if it had been clearer sooner, I might have been a better teacher from the start. More likely, his effect depended on unemulable character or on qualities that he had taken many years to accrue and that no younger man could have reasonably hoped to possess. Born at the turn of the 20th century, he was 59 years old when I showed up in his class and had been teaching at Andover since 1929. His long face crinkled around the eyes and sagged into dewlaps like an elderly hound's. He moved slowly at best and most of the time not at all. Every faculty has its rock stars, but he would have been no one's candidate for the role.

Emory was the anti-Peters, though to a first impression he was scarcely more animated. A heavy, oval Harkness table dominated his classroom. He sat at one end of it with his books and papers spread out before him, twisting and untwisting a rubber band around his fingers as the period progressed. He never stood up or walked around while class was going on, never used the blackboard, never even made more than the most limited gestures with his hands. Everything was words— the words of our texts and the words that we spoke around the table.

The long-time chair of the department in 1959, Emory considered this position an onerous and somewhat annoying duty rather than, as Peters would have, a stepping stone to higher things. After he retired a few years later, one of his would-be successors was said to have been playing pool in a dorm common room when word arrived that he had not been given the job and to have shattered his cue on the edge of the table in vexation. It is impossible to imagine Emory playing pool or caring whether he became department chair or not. Literature, which he knew by heart, abounded in stories of the vanity of human wishes, of men who rode in arrogance up ambition's ferris wheel and were inexorably carried down the other side. And in this case, what a paltry and even masochistic ambition—to have the responsibility of coercing or cajoling a crew of proud, stubborn, contentious colleagues into reaching and keeping agreements about how they were to teach! No, honor required that you do it if the mantle fell on your shoulders, but until then—*be a teacher*.

I became aware of Emory's impatience with his chairmanship only after I had known him for some time. When I was 14, such things meant nothing to me. What did quickly become obvious was his pleasure in the classroom. The crinkles around his eyes had been carved by merriment and each day inscribed them a little more deeply. He liked being there with us, did not hold against us how little we knew, did not imagine that he could, on the timetable of an academic year, cram that void with a file cabinet's worth of designated material and consider his job well done. All those words were too important and too slippery for that. He revered the words in the texts he had chosen, lingered lovingly over the best of them; and he held us accountable for the words we used. But he knew that nothing could be forced, that we could understand only what we could understand.

Many years later a fad for "passion" swept the world of schools. It was supposed to be the quality that distinguished a great teacher. Everyone talked about it and everyone strove to be more passionate than thou. The idea of teachers locked in hot sexual embrace or twisting in terminal agony on a cross would have elicited a whole network of ironic crinkles from Emory. Decorum reigned in his class as in Peters's, though with Emory it was not an artificially imposed order but a natural outgrowth of the one basic condition: he liked being there with us, and he conveyed a sense that he was *all* there, not just professionally there.

Some things about Emory's teaching seem old-fashioned now. He knew and appreciated the moderns, but his sensibility was at bottom Edwardian. Though he understood that Faulkner and Yeats were infinitely greater, he had a weakness for writers like Housman, Galsworthy, and Santayana. Having absorbed my father's nostalgic and sentimental outlook, I was right at home and did not learn until college the dubious lesson that these were minor talents to be scorned. When Emory read us Galsworthy's account of the death of Jolyon Forsyte—how the old man fell asleep in his chair on a summer afternoon and his dog noticed that the thistledown caught on his master's mustache had ceased to move—I felt that Shakespeare himself could hardly have done better.

We wrote constantly, an essay pretty much every week. These came back with scant commentary—an occasional minor correction, a summary phrase or two, a percentage grade. "You write well. 85." Neither Emory nor any other English teacher gave us help or advice between the issuing of the assignment and the turning in of the paper. We wrote; he read, judged, returned; and the cycle began again. I suspect that as he neared the end of his career he was also losing his patience with the incessant paperwork, but his approach was very much the norm, and the young teachers did little more. Today, I lean over my students' shoulders as they write at a computer terminal, encourage them to seek my feedback while the work is in progress. Often I ask them for a draft in the middle of a project and respond with hundreds of words of suggestions. They get the bulk of my response *before* the grade, when they still have motive and opportunity to learn from it by putting it into practice. I am good at offering this help and am usually able to avoid the pitfalls of co-opting or being co-opted. Students—some of them—thank me for the effort I put in. I believe, intuitively, that my system is rich and flexible, that it is perfectly tailored to the individual needs of each student on each assignment, that it is real teaching. I justify the scores of hours that it costs me by telling myself that anything less would be a dereliction. Yet many students, even the thankful ones, seem strangely unable to use what I give them. And I wonder how I learned to write from someone who spent so little time with my writing. One answer is that he simply knew how to make me want to write well. There was a sleight of hand in his way with us, a leverage that operated without being seen.

Emory was the anti-Harrison, too. He detested the athletic machine and all its works, regarded sports as the apotheosis of mindless brutality and the antithesis of the intellectual culture that should be the core of education. "School spirit," to him, was an apprentice form of the boosterism that he deplored when we read *Babbitt* together. Other teachers played along with the jockocracy to various extents, jollying star athletes with allusions to their exploits on the field or introducing sports metaphors into the discourse. *Odysseus is like a quarterback, skilled at reading complex defenses and inventing trick plays; Ajax is like a fullback, sent in to grind out a yard or two in a key situation.* Emory remained aloof from such stuff. There was, in fact, a touch of the maiden aunt about him. He had never married and seemed to hold sexuality of any kind in low regard. Of certain characters in contemporary fiction he remarked disdainfully that "they cohabit like goats." I could get on board with this sort of disdain (which in my case was the surface expression of both deep fear and deep yearning), and I so revered Emory that I successfully repressed in his presence my ongoing flirtation with the athletic program. He was gentle and patient with everyone regardless, but he did, without ever ranting, make his antipathies known, and some of my classmates held them against him. The same boy who later complained that he had never heard a kind or encouraging word from an Andover coach apparently didn't like to hear other adults question robust male values; he once sat with a group of us at a snack bar table and pronounced that "Basford is a cynical, senile dink." Though the Law of Unintended Consequences tells us that we can never know where our teaching goes, we can be quite sure that some students will adore and some despise us (and some both adore *and* despise us) for reasons of their own.

Emory had been master of a dormitory for many years before buying a small house on the outskirts of town—one which commanded, ironically, a panoramic view of the athletic fields. In the dorm he had lived a Spartan existence. The apartment there lacked a kitchen and, liking to entertain, he had had to cook for dinner parties on a hot plate and wash the dishes in the bathtub. After such Spartan quarters, the house must have seemed a well-earned reward, and he arranged it exactly to his specifications. It had dark, lustrous paneling, floor-to-ceiling bookcases, and a small but beautiful flower garden that he tended himself. At the beginning of each school year, he made it known to all his classes that they were invited for tea every Sunday afternoon.

Tea with Emory had the features of a religious observance—mere flimflam to the skeptical, a sacrament to the faithful. The tea was English, the little sandwiches (cucumber or cream cheese and ginger) were English, the books in those tall shelves, the flowers in the garden when we sat outside on a warm fall or spring day were English, English, English. In my senior year, having decided that an English teacher was what I would become and signed up for Emory's renowned American Literature course, I hiked out there almost every Sunday. There were usually half a dozen of us. Little remains to me of what we talked about, though Emory at home was more open about his differences with the school than he was in class. What does remain is the sense of being taken seriously by an adult and being welcomed into a world of adult tastes, adult conversation, adult concerns. He enjoyed being there with us. If he had written a thousand words at the bottom of every paper, he could not have given me anything half so precious.

# Chapter 5

⚌

# PLAY

*ANDOVER AGAIN, 1965. Four years after graduating from boarding school (and a mere three months after breaking the family drought on graduating from college), I am back on the other side of the desk. At Harvard, I have read many books, written many papers, attended many classes and cut more than a few, and even made my first stumbling advances toward the opposite sex. But nothing I have learned in that gaudy palace of intellectual self-esteem has prepared me for this moment. I am a 21-year-old "Teaching Fellow" without the slightest idea how to teach. Despite this ignorance— despite the fact that I am armed only with the wish to be a teacher and not with a single strategy for getting through so much as a single class period, let alone for helping students emerge from it with more skills and knowledge than they brought in—despite my manifest unreadiness for the part in which I've been cast, or chosen to cast myself, here I am. No script, no rehearsals, no direction. The curtain rises, the audience settles expectantly, and you begin to…what?*

*Fortunately, today, the first day of all, there's a bit of practical business to be taken care of—collecting $2 from each student for a sheaf of mimeoed* *grammar lessons that my elders in the department have prepared. Most of the boys have their money at hand in bills, but the last in line, a new boy with the intriguing name of Johnson Lightfoote, intends to pay in coin, chiefly pennies, which he begins to count out slowly and earnestly onto my desk.*

*I'm tempted to let him go on and on, filling in at least a few minutes of the dreadful abyss of time that stretches before me. What else do I have planned? My own boring freshman English teacher Donald Peters with his minutely prepared note cards begins to look like a role model.*

*"...thirty-five, forty, forty-one, forty-two, forty-three..."*

*I raise my palm in the stop-traffic position and pitch my tone somewhere between sardonic and gruff, the combined voices of W. C. Fields and John Wayne: "I trust you, Lightfoote."*

*There is a ripple of not unfriendly laughter. Empty time still yawns, but I have done two things that, as I will learn in the years to come, a teacher must do. I have improvised to meet the unexpected. And I have made my first classroom joke.*

Teaching, as I gradually learned, is play, and anyone, at whatever level, who forgets this axiom will probably have a sorry time of it. It is play in the sense that surfing is play—students' energy cresting in a big comber that can either give you an exhilarating ride to the beach or dump you and pound you to the bottom with a mouthful of sand and salt. It is like a tennis game, where the pleasure comes from the long rallies, the angles, the gets, the changes of pace and spin—and above all from the sense of being evenly matched. People who try to serve an ace every time don't make good teachers even if they can crank their delivery up to 130 mph. Yes, I can be Roger Federer to your teenage wannabe, but you will learn nothing from watching my cannonballs fly by.

One winning feature of play is that nothing bad can happen. There are no failed experiments. All is there both to be enjoyed for its own sake and to be learned from. But, paradoxically, play is also about risk—the teacher's risk, too. I must be willing—even happy—to face the fact that I can't control everything, can't know everything, can't prepare for everything, can't expect perfection, am going to lose some of the games. The risk is what makes the experience real and alive for everyone in the room. From their built-in position of weakness, students take a risk every time they walk in the door. Unless my risk approaches theirs, the air goes out of the ball we are playing with.

Unfortunately, I must learn this lesson over and over because, although I understand the logic and power of it, it is not native to me. Instead, my reflex is to micromanage. My methodical father with his horror of disorder and his unbreachable sense of process keeps looking over my shoulder: let's not get ahead of ourselves. But the truth is that if we don't get ahead of ourselves, we won't get *anywhere*. What is education if not a determined push to get ahead of ourselves, to reach beyond what we can grasp? I know this, but a bureaucracy inside me keeps demanding the paperwork. Once, years along, when I should have known better, my own impulse to settle procedures and establish boundaries expressed itself too ponderously on the first day of school and I ruined an entire course. *This is the late-paper policy. These are the consequences of plagiarism. Here's how you are to lay out your essays.* Straight through to June the kids sat as if pinned to the backstop, dazed, not even bothering to flail at what I sent their way. I remember the peculiar cold sweat that broke out in the small of my back every day when I realized anew that nothing would be coming back from the other side of the net.

One way I learned to try to keep myself from over-preparing is to limit my notes to the merest possible outline, a sketch map of our route through the 45 minutes we have together today. If it doesn't fit comfortably on a half-sheet of letter-size paper, it's too much. There has to be blank space around the edges for the improvisation and the laughter. If we veer away at checkpoint 2 out of 5, so be it. If we don't get to the end, all the better—something is left for tomorrow, something that gains a tiny increment of secret momentum from having been planned

BE A TEACHER

for but not accomplished today. Going deeper trumps going forward. Less is more.

Except for the laughter—for the laughter, more is more. We cannot remind ourselves too often that everything we do totters on the edge of comedy and that comedy is redemptive. The joke's on you and me, on Hamlet and Holden, on the bum sentence with the unintended meaning. It's on one kid's disheveled late entrance when she has overslept and on another's unaccustomed cheerfulness when he has overdosed on caffeine. It's on my blank look when someone mentions a pop star better known than the president to everyone else at the table.

One morning in the late 70's at the Cambridge School of Weston, the joke was on the Head as she stood up to wield her doubtful authority in assembly. Some outrage or other had to be addressed, one that among the daily outrages of Cambridge School life must have seemed over the top. The community had to understand that whatever it was was harmful to the reputation of…was dangerous to…was unacceptable in… Behind her, out of the gloom in the empty end of the gymnasium, a person-sized cylindrical shape with feet appeared, dancing and gyrating as it drew nearer. It was made of pink papier-maché striped here and there with writhing purple veins. Helen, purposefully oblivious, smitten with the righteousness of the message that she had to deliver, continued her admonitions, and the audience held its breath. At length, the dance intensified to a frenzy and the top of the tube erupted in a magnificent plume of shaving cream. Gravitas subverted again.

We should probably teach as if there's a dancing phallus behind us all the time, a subversive id to our prim, pompous superegos—our dreams of eradicating pronoun reference errors, banishing rogue apostrophes, grappling every paragraph to the thesis statement with hoops of steel, fixing on pins the image patterns in *Paradise Lost*. A word of the moment in discussions of educational policy is *intentional*, as in "we need to lay out our scope-and-sequence in a more intentional way." To help us achieve this we employ consultants and strategic planners who have won their spurs making corporations a tenth of a percent more efficient, so that they can stay competitive in what we are assured is an entirely new 21$^{st}$-century environment, one where no one can afford, even for an instant, to take his eye off the ball. In this strenuously grim climate I have to keep reminding myself to turn up the dial on frivolity. We are not manufacturing can openers here but sharing a few precious hours with grumpy, cheerful, feisty, querulous, randy, reflective, impulsive, generous, and spirited teenagers, who deserve a full initiation into the human comedy before they go to college, let alone law school.

The play's the thing, says that grumpy adolescent Hamlet, trying to make himself more intentional. He's been fooling around too long. Now he wants to use a theatrical performance for practical purposes—a piece of police work. Nothing here about the word's shared roots with Middle Dutch *pleien*, which means to leap for joy, dance, be glad: the point of this show is to drive a stake into the stepfather's heart. But at least what Hamlet intends is human, if not humane. He's not trying to run up a profit margin.

The classroom is a theater that needs to be lit every day. Another current educational maxim holds that the teacher must be the "guide at your side," not the "sage on the stage," but there's a great deal to be said for teacher as performer. I think of some thrilling lecturers in college and graduate school: Harvey Goldberg replaying the collapse of internationalism in 1914 so dramatically that 300 of us sat there gasping at the tragedy of it and of the holocaust to come; Walter Jackson Bate assuming and projecting the great, tormented soul of Samuel Johnson. My own usually brief performances run to the comic and tend to be ad-libbed. I ignore Hamlet's warning about clowns who speak "more than is set down for them…though in the meantime some necessary question of the play be then to be considered." Necessary questions? Here he does sound too much like a management consultant laying down rules to make the troupe run lean.

Most of the performing, though, must be done by the students, and they must do a lot of it. They have to get the words of literature into their bodies—chests, mouths, and hands. They have to get their own thoughts into spoken words, so that the act of speaking can pull more thoughts out of them. School mistakenly privileges the cerebral over the visceral, writing over speaking. It wants everything buttoned up, nailed down, intentional—no half-formed judgments, no emotional leaks, no loose talk; all must be in black and white so that we can look back over it and probe for the weak spots, tighten the connections. The machine will run smoothly so long as there is no play in the moving parts.

I am listening eagerly for emotional leaks when my Milton sophomores stand up to perform. Some who cannot write a critical essay to save their lives can show understanding that goes straight to the heart. Juliana's voice makes poignant the tragic irony of the pilots in Randal Jarrell's "Losses," who flew "bombers named for girls" and "burned the cities we had learned about in school." (This is Juliana, who on any given day may or may not have learned about any cities because she may or may not have done her homework.) Bonnie fearlessly summons all the viciousness of too-long-delayed recrimination in Plath's "Daddy" and punctuates the last line—"I'm through"—by dashing her script to the floor. (This is Bonnie, who wept when she got back her midyear exam.) Roger, monologuing from *Macbeth*, holds a flashlight under his chin to suggest a witch's wrinkled features, then stabs its beam quizzically in front of him as he tries to trace the illusory progress of an air-borne dagger. (Roger is still piqued with me for dismissing too summarily his unfounded interpretation of a poem, but my effusive admiration for his *Macbeth* performance takes some of the edge off. Two years later, he is back for a full course on Shakespeare.)

Play in the performance sense is deeply involving. You *can* give it less than everything, but like a missing tooth the gap will show in a particularly public way. Write an unmeant essay and after a quick trip through the teacher's grading machine it slips inconspicuously into file cabinet or trash can. Give an unmeant performance and lots of people are going to notice. Audiences motivate with a sharpness that teachers can't equal. Instead of having to give the assignment, urge it through to completion, and then judge it (a hermetically sealed loop that seems arbitrary and artificial), I can count on the prospect of an audience to make students want to perform well and can become their ally in reaching for that goal. The whole project seems natural and real. *You don't understand that line, and everyone is going to know it. You don't feel that line, and no one else is going to feel it either.* These compelling messages take academic life as close as it is going to get to the marvelously self-correcting world of competitive games. When I was coaching chess, I would reiterate ad nauseam the obvious theoretical truth that it's better not to leave your King in the middle of the board, but only when a player had been burned by doing it three or four times did the lesson get learned. The game did the teaching.

Sometimes what you have to play is hardball. "The text does not support that interpretation," you have to say. Or, "The paper is late and it goes down one grade." Or, "You botched the end of the last project and I'm not giving any quarter on the end of this one." Whenever I say these things, a shadow of guilt passes over my mind: I worry that I am becoming another cog in the factory system. Foreman Dave. But I do say them, and I tell myself, with good reason, that having a system in place is actually one of the preconditions for successful play. A school without edges is a school without a center, and we need to remember that—as long as we don't become so obsessed with maintaining the edges that we forget about the center they're there to protect. If you come to class—game on. If you don't—game off. And please try to bring something good with you when you come. I am irritated at Trudi, who has been mailing in her rehearsals for a class performance of the *Odyssey*. She stumbles over the words, slumps listlessly, stifles a yawn. Some Calypso! I send her a scathing note. The rehearsals improve, and when showtime comes she radiates the goddess's seductive wiles and is justifiably pleased with herself, grateful for my prodding. On the last day of the year, embarrassed to give me a hug in front of her classmates, she slips back in to do it after the others have left.

Teaching is sweaty work, too, and there are times every year—and have been whole years in my life as a teacher—when I am afraid the work has made me a very dull boy. There is the cold sweat when a class has gone dead and you sit there mortified with failure and striving with desperate futility to breathe a little life back into it. In the worst case, as when I sent out the wrong signals on Day One, this kind of sweat starts trickling at the beginning of every subsequent period, before you've even had a chance to say hello. You know what isn't coming. There is also the warmer and happier sweat worked up when so much is going on that you can't stay abreast of it. Hands wave on all sides, people are blurting, a tangential conversation breaks out, the air fills with questions that aren't getting addressed, points that aren't getting developed. Opportunities for teacher intervention multiply bewilderingly. Someone who habitually talks too much gets the floor and begins a monologue that threatens to damp the whole thing down like a carbon rod in a reactor pile. While you are waiting for an access point that will permit you to cut her off more or less kindly—she's smart, she penetrates to a level the others can't get to by themselves, you *need* her—you realize that one line of the conversation derailed itself into a fatal misunderstanding five minutes ago and you'll somehow have to get back there and reroute. And then you see out of the corner of your eye (because he has intentionally sat where he will not be in your crosshairs) that a boy who almost never talks is stirring with an incipient idea—what are the chances of pulling him in? And suppose you do—what if he heads off down the false trail, has to be corrected, and sinks permanently into his inhibitions? Hopefully, vigorously, you wield your baton, and on a good day you coax this wheezing, dissonant orchestra to some semblance of harmony. Work and play coalesce. You have to unzip the fleece vest you wore on this cold morning. After they're gone, you have to go out to the fountain in the hall for a drink.

Most of the dull-boy work of teaching, the part that threatens to crush your soul, is done when the students aren't there. While they, you resentfully suspect, are enjoying water fights in the dormitory or playing Zombie Alert on their Xbox for the 300th time, you are burning the midnight oil. Midnight has always been about my limit, and it is late enough. I felt both awe and pity toward a former colleague who would over and over again get inundated so deeply that he had to pull an all-nighter every month or so in order to get his nose back above the water line. Unhealthy obsessiveness, certainly—best leave the all-nighters to the students, who can at least derive some romantic frisson from watching dawn break. But still, there is always more that a teacher *could* do. Even if you are scrupulous about not overplanning, you don't want to go in there the next day without your half-sheet— a program to hew to or deviate from as opportunity suggests. Even underplanning takes time. And the preparation is nothing beside the endless Sisyphean cycle of reading and responding to students' papers.

I don't say *correcting*. Correcting is not what I do, or is only a minute part of what I do. Yes, if the modifiers dangle and the pronouns have nothing to refer to, I mark the spot and often send the perpetrator back to reconstruct the sentence. Correcting the errors myself would be throwing sand against the wind, because the chance that my change would register—that the student would notice it, grasp its logic, and recognize the underlying principle that he could then apply to any number of other sentences in his future—is no better than one in a thousand. If I give him a cue and he has to make the change himself, the chance goes up to perhaps one in a hundred, an improvement in odds that may actually justify my having to look at his paper *again* later in the week to make sure that the change he has made is actually a correction.

Marking grammar mistakes is, in any case, the easy part of paper reading, the part that I can do with a quarter of my consciousness, and fast. The hard part, the midnight oil part, is to pick through the whole twisted backlash of thought and expression that all but a few student papers inevitably present. The writer has perhaps read only a part of the book he is writing about and that part with only a quarter of *his* consciousness. He has waited until too late to start the paper and has therefore jumped into writing it without pausing to collect his thoughts. He didn't quite understand the assignment when I laid it out, and now, at his desk at one a.m., he cannot go back to clarify it. If he wants to say anything—and wanting to say something is by no means a given, since he may just be complying dutifully with the fact that he must give me pages of words in the morning—he is not sure of *what* he wants to say. Nevertheless, he begins, hoping that what he wants to say will occur to him as he goes on. This approach, the write-to-learn approach, could pay off handsomely if he had left time to write twice, once for learning and once for communicating the result to me. But he hasn't. Dawn is breaking. Perhaps the urgency concentrates his mind, but more likely he pokes away at the keyboard in a mixed state of panic and intellectual somnambulism, repeating himself, plunging into non-sequiturs, forgetting the subject of a sentence before he gets to the predicate. The paper will arrive on my desk as a one-shot, and he will be able to drowse complacently through the rest of the day, having transferred his anxiety to me.

What am I to do but make sure that my lamp has enough oil in it? I have to get the papers back. A gap of as much as a week between stimulus and response is probably fatal to any shred of possibility that the writer will be able to connect the two and grow by making the connection. So here is my stack—if I am lucky, no further stacks are stacked up behind it for the moment—and each item in the stack of 12 or 14 is a conundrum that might take a whole day for me to solve, if a solution actually exists. I think of my father patiently plucking apart those Gordian knots of fishing line that my sister and I had brought him. I think of the minimalist Emory Basford slashing the knot with a terse "You write well—88" or a "Not your best work—75." And I remember that Emory helped me improve not by correcting what I wrote or even by responding to it more than perfunctorily but by making me (how *did* he do it, exactly?) aspire to be a writer.

Still, I don't have his zen tricks and I can't lay off. Responding is both a duty I feel and a compulsion I can't resist. At the same time, I don't have all day. There's preparation to do for tomorrow, and even now new stacks of paper are being cobbled together at my command, because the squirrel wheel can never stop turning. So I get myself a cup of coffee and clear a space at the table and begin, reckoning that I can spend about 40 minutes on each of these thousand-word essays.

I begin, unfortunately, in much the same way as the hypothetical student writer I described above—without knowing what I want to say. In my case, the question is not of particular content, which of course will vary from paper to paper, but of overall approach. I am going to cram some brief responses—no more than two sentences at a time, at most—into the margins or between the lines of the student's essay; and still, more than 40 years into this work, I have not settled in my mind the essential question of cause and effect. Causes and effects. What *kind* of thing can I write here that will make a difference? I want to clarify the writer's understanding of this assignment and prepare him to deal better with future assignments. I want to help him express himself more pointedly and energetically. I want most of all to help him learn to honor his writing by meaning it. But what always makes me hesitate on the verge of one more stack is the awareness that I almost certainly will never know whether what I write has any of these intended consequences. Responding to papers is like all teaching in this respect: a wish that is unlikely to yield any tangible fulfillment. Progress is slow and often goes underground. It may show up as a tiny quartz outcrop for next year's teacher or erupt volcanically for a college professor five years down the line. It may be recalled with gratitude at the 20th reunion—or is that just nostalgia talking?

I must begin (40 minutes apiece, and now the first five have gone in wool-gathering), so I write the two kinds of thing that, after all this time with all these many stacks, seem best to me: encouragement and questions. The encouragement is easy enough to deliver—*good, well argued, yes*—but not always so easy to find an occasion for. I often resort to grasping at whatever feeble straw presents itself, perhaps a single incisive phrase protruding from an immense dung heap of empty bluster. *Nice point!* The questions flow more naturally and sincerely: *What does this mean? Why do you think so? How do you know? Aren't you contradicting what you said up above?* On the whole, I have more faith in the questions. As a response, they invite a further response. They put what would otherwise lie dead on the page back in play, make the reading of the paper a little more like what might happen in class. If paper after paper raises the same set of questions, I can actually take them back into class for more talk. Meanwhile, 40 minutes apiece; and whatever game I try to make of it, however much I would like to imagine that a dialogue is going on, what's happening here is not play. It is work.

Several decades after Johnson Lightfoote counted out his pennies, I am curled up in the shadows under my classroom table, waiting for a class of seventh-graders to arrive. Yesterday one of them, a burr-headed, puppyish kid who in fact recently wrote a series of ingratiating poems about his family's new puppy, hid down here until I had begun the class. Just as I was asking, "Has anyone seen Mike?" he popped out amid roars of delight.

His coup must be answered, at whatever cost to dignity. Not that I have much dignity left—already on the file cabinet there is a photo of me dancing on the top of this same table in fulfillment of an idle promise made early one year, when the prospect of having to keep it on the last day seemed far off. And this is middle school, where dignity, as Grant Swartley's rooster jump proved long ago, takes a distant second place to drama.

Someone arrives early, sees my toes sticking out, and peers down into the gloom. I lock eyes with him and put a finger to my lips. *Don't betray me.* Even if he does, they'll still have that pleasure. But he doesn't. The others bustle in, squawking, shoving, and slamming their overloaded bookbags thunderously on the table top. I wait a few beats for my absence to be felt. When the sound of puzzlement seems right, I slither, not very nimbly, up and into my empty seat. Applause. The maneuver is a complete success. The day they graduate from high school some of them still want to reminisce with me about that time in seventh grade when I came out from under the table.

# Chapter 6

———✦✦———

# AUTHORITY

*MADISON, WISCONSIN, 1966—A bright fall day. I have come west in pursuit of two things, a girl and a Master's degree. The relationship dissolved a couple of months before I even got to town; the degree seems likely to happen without requiring 100% of my intellectual energy. Since I intend to get back into a classroom of my own as soon as possible, I am on the lookout for fields of knowledge that might be applicable, and learning something about how the mind works seems like a good idea. So here I am in a featureless auditorium in the Psychology building, auditing Psych 101.*

*Psych 101 is taught entirely on television—a dozen small screens lining the walls of this sterile space. The teachers, never the same one twice, appear solely as talking heads, purveyors of a curriculum completely stripped of color and personality. I've been making a game attempt to follow along; perhaps I can even break new ground for the Smith men by learning something about how my own mind works. But the material is dry, the medium is alienating, and I am hardly surprised this morning when, after a brief ruckus in the back of the hall, masked guerillas come storming down the aisles and begin yanking the plugs of the monitors out of their sockets. No one resists and no one plugs the TV's back in when the masked men have fled. There are no adults to intervene. Instead, we all stand up and wander out into the sunshine.*

That fall, when I arrived in Madison, a single, tremendous issue obsessed the national consciousness and also mine. The issue was authority—who held it, how it had been obtained, whether it was deserved, how it might be challenged. The country was in an uproar over the war in Vietnam. Lyndon Johnson's tired, dewlapped face and Texas cornpone accent had acquired the ability to drive people my age into a fury of rebelliousness. What gave this aging cracker the right to send young people halfway around the world for the purpose of killing and being killed in someone else's country?

Any academic town worth its salt is given to challenging the status quo, and in towns set amid a hundred thousand acres of cornfield or cattle ranch the challenge often becomes especially strident. Madison fizzed with revolt. Graffiti on a construction fence in the middle of town gave voice to the zeitgeist: *Lock up MacNamara and throw away the Ky.* (There was also the mock indignant *Who screwed Fillmore out of Mount Rushmore?*—a jeer at the pretensions of all leadership, past and present.) After remaining steadfastly apolitical in my undergraduate years, I snorted this heady atmosphere and found it good. Or at least intoxicating. If the girl I had followed here didn't reciprocate my feelings, there were plenty of others who might. The air was full of hope. And with a great transformation looming, there was no time to brood over the merely personal.

On Saturday mornings in Madison, I would wake up in my drafty, down-at-heel studio apartment, pull on my clothes, and walk three quarters of a mile down Langdon Street to the university bookstore. Occasionally I would need a book for my English courses, but most of the time I was seeking fodder for a reading program of my own. I was enthralled with the history of revolution.

Unlike Intro to Psych, history had teachers with three dimensions.

The agent of my infatuation was Harvey Goldberg, whose course on Europe during and after World War I attracted overflow crowds in the enormous old lecture hall where he gave it. Students perched on window ledges, flocked the steps up to the stage, just sat down in the aisles. Many of them must have been auditors, like me, drawn from their routine encounters with math or language, perhaps even from ministering to the prize cows in the agricultural division up the road. We gravitated to Goldberg with a sense that what we would be hearing from him about the agonies of 50 years before offered lessons for the better future that we imagined would be emerging soon. We shared a bliss-is-it-in-this-dawn-to-be-alive feeling, a kind of rapture that Wordsworth wrote about in *The Prelude*, where he described his time in France during the years after the storming of the Bastille. Reading the poem for my course on the Romantics—whose flouting of the establishment made it seem my only English course with any pertinence—I contrived to miss the tempering perspective of Wordsworth's past tense. He was thinking back on his youth in France from a later time when everything had gone wrong, when the ecstatic energy of '89 had subverted itself and "a Pope was summoned in to crown an Emperor." In 1967, what we felt was the bliss. We did not foresee Nixon and Kissinger, much less Reagan, still less George W. Bush or Donald Trump.

Goldberg strode stiffly and almost maniacally around the stage, as if he could scarcely contain the pent-up force of the tales he had to tell. He gave the initials of French labor organizations—CGT, SFIO—an incantatory power. He had written a book about Jean Jaurès, the socialist whose assassination in July, 1914, ended all hope that an international brotherhood of workers could keep Europe from spiraling into war. Goldberg was also an expert on Rosa Luxemburg—Red Rosa— who survived the war years in a German prison, emerged into the chaos of November, 1918, and was brutally murdered and dumped into a canal by reactionaries the following January. Luxemburg enthralled me with her fierce refusal to compromise. I adopted her as a kindred spirit, the Red Rosa to my Red Smith. When a friend on the outside wrote to apologize for not being radical enough, Rosa replied that insufficient radicalism was not the problem—that in fact the friend was not radical *at all*, and that when she, Rosa, should be released from her cell, she would hunt down such flabby liberals "with trumpets, whips, and bloodhounds." Goldberg held us spellbound with these stories, often running long past the end of one class period and into the next. No one ever moved a muscle. No one thought—at least I certainly didn't—that the roles in the narrative might be reversed, that we ourselves might be the ones pursued by the pack and end up floating in the frigid water of a bleak industrial canal. Bliss was it in that dawn to be alive.

Each week I hauled a load of history books back to my apartment house, carried them through the entryway that stank of spilled beer and up stairs along which half the banister spindles had been kicked out by the people who drank what they managed not to spill. Across the hall from me lived a guy from Janesville who routinely woke up on weekend mornings so hung over that he could not remember where he had left his motorcycle the night before. In another apartment resided a sophisticated easterner, a couple of years older than I was, whose grandfather had been a famous novelist and playwright; he was sublimely detached not only from the frat lifestyle but also from politics. Upstairs was a boy who all but clicked his heels and saluted whenever General William Westmoreland appeared on TV to claim that the body-counts were favorable and that the United States was making "progress" in Vietnam. I was friendly with all my housemates and did not stop to reflect that if they were a representative cross-section of my age-group, revolution could not be in the immediate future. Instead, I propped myself up on my bed and read about Lenin, Trotsky, and Stalin and about the Freikorps and the rise of Hitler.

Many of the English professors did little better than cathode ray tubes, and I rather quickly began to suspect that further study in this field led inexorably into a cul de sac where one would certainly lose his manhood and very possibly his life. My Milton teacher was dead on arrival—a youngish man who hunched over his podium and droned about the influence of Ariosto and made us write criticism of criticism until the rolling organ music of *Paradise Lost* faded and disappeared behind a dry static hiss. Ricardo Quintana, who had been teaching the Age of Swift since the 1930's, had never come to terms with the existence of Freudian psychology and its possible bearing on his subject. That Swift had an obsessive interest in shit Quintana flatly denied, all but literally clapping his hands over his ears and steering us quickly away from the passages that made this fascination plain. Fie on scatology. He preferred to talk about such "capital verses" as "A Description of the Morning"—he actually used the word "capital," as if he were sunk in a leather chair at a London club and savoring the day's cricket results or a particularly good single-malt scotch. Quintana was the biggest name in the country in 18th-century studies. To me, he looked like the archetype of mummified authority, the dead hand of the past clinging grimly to a little hoard of useless information and stale, dishonest ideas.

A year later, I came to Racine, to the Prairie School, with these images—the inspired, inspiring Goldberg, the moribund Quintana— fresh in my mind and little practical knowledge about either how to emulate the one or avoid becoming the other. I was at least partly aware that I had faked my way through my Andover internship. Now I had my advanced degree but didn't know what it was good for—it seemed like just the sort of paper credential that would soon be swept like the Mensheviks into the dustbin of history. My jaundiced view of authority, feeding off the national questions on the subject, came at an awkward time for me as I entered a profession in which authority was, or at least had been, the primary stock in trade. Uncle Doug Crate had had nothing to offer *but* authority—neither well founded knowledge, nor ideas, nor even intellectual appetite of any kind. He simply turned up the volume and battered you into submission. John Colby at Andover had come by his authority more honestly—he knew all there was to know about Latin grammar and poetry, could scan a line of Virgil in his sleep, had transmuted the fine points of syntax into mnemonics with driving rhythms that had the force of immutable law. *Si, nisi, num, and ne--*, we chanted, *every ali- drops away.* And *the dative of the agent with the passive periphrastic.* But if questioned, he reared back at once onto the throne of unquestionability, as I saw him do one day when he forgot the name of a student, was reminded of it in saucy tones by another boy, flew into a towering rage, and dismissed the class summarily before any more embarrassing holes in his memory could be exposed. Even the gentle Emory Basford relied on the authority that hung about him as naturally as his professorial tweeds: he never needed to bully or explode, he did draw you as best he could toward a grown up independence, but he was still the shaping force in every transaction.

I looked into myself and saw no such force. Seeing none, I began in compensation to doubt whether authority was central to teaching and then, as doubt hardened quickly into dogma, to assert zealously that it was not. This subversive position would have qualified me for a job at Summerhill, the utopian English school described in a book that a friend had given me in Madison and that supplied me abundantly with talking points. At Prairie School, however, it soon became problematic.

Prairie had existed for only two years in 1967. It was the brain-child of Sam Johnson, the head of the Johnson's Wax Corporation, and his wife Imogene, who wanted a place to educate their children without sending them away to boarding school. The Johnsons' concept of school creation was more or less to add money and stir. Prairie sprang rapidly out of nothing on a patch of flat, windswept land along the shores of Lake Michigan north of town. Frank Lloyd Wright had designed the family's nearby home and the company's famous headquarters in downtown Racine. Now Wright was dead, but his associates were laying out the school in complementary style, elegant intersecting arcs of brickwork faced with large, curved windows that admitted sunlight and afforded panoramic views of the surrounding emptiness. New construction followed new construction, and the fall I came a wing had just been completed to accommodate the first high school students as

Prairie grew toward its ultimate K-12 configuration. As I drove in, a couple of days before classes were to start, tractors with spray attachments lumbered back and forth applying the finishing touch, a coat of instant grass.

All this rawness looked like an opportunity, and Prairie's headmaster Jack Mitchell, as he had hired me that spring, had sold it as one. I would be working, with others, to build something entirely new—a worthy project for a young man with new ideas. Jack didn't inquire too closely about what those ideas were, and I was too caught up in my visions to reflect that a school without a history might be especially resistant to innovative arrangements and might instead make fabricating a past for itself its first order of business. Nor, in my pleasure at escaping the Madison lit-crit mill, did I notice as more than a passing shadow one fact that might have stopped me cold: that, since Prairie was a wholly-owned subsidiary of the wax works, I would be drawing my small paycheck straight from one of the bastions of American capitalism. All private schools serve in collusion with and at the pleasure of the plutocracy, but in more established ones the relationship tends to be discreetly veiled. At Prairie it was as naked as the landscape and should, if I had been seriously interested in creating a new world order, have given me more pause than it did. Wanting to be a teacher more than I wanted to start a revolution, I chose to live with the cognitive dissonance that, in one form or another, is almost everyone's most serviceable and durable dodge; and I have lived with it ever since. Recently I was both pleased and amused to learn that someone had referred to me as a "Bolshevik" during a dispute with Milton Academy about unionizing the faculty. I liked the flutter that this designation seemed to stir in the opposing ranks. "Red" Smith rides again! But if I had really been a Bolshevik, I would have abandoned teaching forty years ago.

Prairie was no Summerhill and was not about to be. Jack knew what the Johnsons wanted and laid on the traditions as fast as those tractors laid on the fake grass. He himself was part of the desired eastern prep aura, having been lured, after an extended courtship, from a school in Maine where he had been contentedly serving as head. What finally won him, he said, was the promise of a free hand, but his hand busied itself chiefly with things like choosing the school colors, composing the school song, and designing the school uniform. Freedom, I thought, ought to be used to promote more freedom, and these projects of Jack's were at best tangential to the cause of developing a free school.

The last of them actually ran counter to the cause. Uniforms were what soldiers wore, and the point of a school was to produce people who would challenge the ill-founded authority to which soldiers blindly submitted. Driven by the kind of intemperate rhetoric that I have always enjoyed a little too much (did we want our kids to form jackbooted ranks like those that strutted past the reviewing stand at Nuremburg? and so forth), the uniform question became heated. When I and some other young teachers pressed the point, Jack called a faculty meeting. What it came down to, he informed us, was this: "If you work for General Motors and General Motors tells you to wear a celluloid collar, you wear a celluloid collar." I recognized "General Motors" as a polite substitute for Johnson's Wax, and whatever a celluloid collar might be I regarded being told to wear one as a form of tyranny. Jack would have his way for now, but his position looked weak. I pictured him in one of my favorite scenes from the movie of *Doctor Zhivago*: a Russian officer climbs on a barrel to address mutinous troops and has almost succeeded in calming them when the top of the barrel breaks and plunges him into waist-deep water. Then they shoot him and continue with the mutiny.

Unfortunately, the barrel *I* was standing on did not look much sturdier. Just as most tsarist army officers owed their ranks solely to their status as aristocrats, my own qualifications as a teacher were unrelated to any demonstrable aptitude for the job. To my credit were eight years of study at eastern schools whose names everyone knew—a first-class ride on the conveyor belt that began with Meadowbrook. In promoting Prairie to parents who wanted their children's education to have a certain cachet, Jack could take these associations to the bank. But when the time came to get into the classroom, I still had only the sketchiest idea of what to do there. I had been given four different courses to teach, a staggering load for someone who had never before tried to teach more than a single course at a time. The weight of the preparations oppressed me. Though I had an appetite for hard work and swotted away like a monk in my squalid one-room apartment, I couldn't find the necessary rhythm to alternate low-prep and high-prep activities and keep things from piling up. In fact, I didn't really know any low-prep activities. The essence of teaching is to make the students do 90% of the work, because they learn by doing it, not by listening to you talk about it. If I had grasped this basic principle, I would have been a better teacher as well as a less-harried one. But teaching-as-talking was mostly what I had seen and what I thought was required of me.

Some of the students were very ready to listen and, as I learned to make room for their responses, to respond. Racine and its downscale southerly neighbor, Kenosha, lay at the heart of what two academics in a Richard Russo novel refer to as "the mid-fucking-west" and had something of the flavor of Sherwood Anderson's Winesburg. Squalid, dull, and void of sentient life as they seemed, they were full of people who chafed at the provincialism and could hardly wait to get away from it. Prairie looked like a way out to these dreamers, and I, with my talk of books and ideas, sounded like a voice from the other side. Though some J-Wax executives' children fit this profile too, most of the would-be escapees came from among the scholarship kids that the school took on out of dutiful benevolence, not recognizing that they alone would save it from mediocrity. To them—to Pam and Jeff, Dru and David and Marty—I was a good teacher already, not because I knew much about how to teach but because I represented what they had been hoping for and made those hopes seem a little more plausible. Perhaps, in truth, there is no more valuable teacher function than as a lightning rod for hopes. In any case, they more than repaid me by making me feel successful, or at least wishing me success. As I stumbled around precariously on my barrel-top, I could be sure they were not among those rooting for that too-thin surface to give way.

Others would certainly have enjoyed the spectacle of any teacher brought low; and since I, to bolster my shaky confidence, put on a strenuous show of authoritative zeal, my downfall would have been all the more entertaining. My experience at Andover, both as student and as apprentice teacher, had not prepared me for the kind of overt resistance I was now encountering. Resistance is inevitable, but at Andover the weight of the institution drove it underground, where it hid beneath a screen of insincere yes-sir's and no-sir's. Prairie was a private school, too, but a weightless one, so tenuous and new that it could offer teachers very little backup. I was on my own and a target of opportunity for kids like Kathleen and her sister Connie, who seemed bent on rejecting, deflecting, or subverting whatever I had to offer. These two had apparently hijacked a truck loaded with cosmetics and decided to use up the swag before it could be reclaimed. In their full warpaint of powder and kohl and mascara, they looked like a pair of sassy raccoons, who, if cornered, would bite. Wearing a uniform didn't bother them— the regulation skirt length was two inches above the knee, but they just rolled up their waistbands to expose an extra six inches of thigh. They skillfully varied their delivery in order to keep me off balance. One moment they would be outright insolent, the next flirtatious, and then sullen and unresponsive. They spent more time in the bathroom adjusting their getup than they did in class. Kathleen was very smart but had no interest in developing that side of her character. She was having too much fun gaming the new teacher, who barked loudly and nipped at her heels but couldn't keep her from moving off in whatever direction she pleased.

There was a further turn of the screw: I undermined my own authority coming and going, both because I was so awkwardly eager to establish it and because I philosophically did not believe in having it at all. Summerhill taught that people will not learn anything until they choose for themselves to learn it and that the requirements of traditional schools are at best inefficient and at worst damaging to the organic growth of young minds. Accepting this theory as truth, I expended a great deal of energy trying to make students believe that my lessons were not compulsory and that force had no place in education. Exactly how I squared this message with the fact that I was assigning homework and scolding them if they didn't do it was not clear at the time and has not become clearer since. Perhaps the self-contradictory nature of my economic arrangements (revolutionary thinker and running dog of the wax establishment) softened me up for other self-contradictions. Cognitive dissonance can be catching, and as the anti-father in the father position, I was constantly tripping over my own cross purposes.

"Why did you give us this assignment?" a boy who had been paying careful attention to my pronouncements on progressive educational precepts once asked.

"Because I want to force you to think for yourselves," I blurted.

A gotcha grin appeared on his face. "Force?" he said.


My neophyte's skirmish with the idea of authority was about 95% pure confusion, a fog of battle in which I improvised field expedients as I went along, without ever getting a comprehensive view of the terrain or the troops. I could and often did shift in a trice from a model of the most supine permissiveness to a petty tyrant of almost Crate-like dimensions. The surprising thing is that I enjoyed myself so much in the process. To those back home who asked how I was doing, I described Prairie's many faults and minimized my own; I also said, truthfully, that I loved my work. Here, too, I should point out that I was only 95% confused and that a small portion of my consciousness was already coming to understand, however dimly, one critical point about education: that the balance of authority actually does reside with the student and that a teacher who denies or resists this fact (as many do) risks reducing himself to irrelevance.

Students hold ultimate authority for two reasons. One is simply that they are the future. They are younger than you are, and after you are gone they will still be here, bull-headedly making the mistakes you warned them against and otherwise flouting the brilliant lessons that you spent so much time preparing for them. The second reason, more important than this biological and chronological certainty of being supplanted, goes straight to the philosophical core of the business: the mind is and must remain free. As soon as we forget this principle, we have given up teaching and begun indoctrinating.

Nowhere is intellectual freedom more important than in the humanities, and especially in English, the subject with the softest edges and the most room for argument. The Quadratic Formula remains the Quadratic Formula whether we like it or not, and we have little choice in how to interpret it. The same cannot be said of *Hamlet*, which does not even have a single stable text that everyone can agree on. What Shakespeare wrote is irretrievably lost, muddled forever during his lifetime by improvising actors, hasty copyists, printers of varying competence, and pirates who worked from memory to hustle out their own editions, and later by the efforts of subsequent editors to repair these damages. To be an authority on the text of *Hamlet* is to know just how much we cannot know. And when we move to interpretation and evaluation, true subjective chaos blooms. It is fair to tell students that hundreds of millions of people have regarded *Hamlet* as the pinnacle of English literature, but we must also ask them to plug their ears against the roar of this reputation and decide for themselves what they think of the play. Stepping nimbly out of the way so that they can decide what they think of it is the zen move in teaching *Hamlet* or any other literary work—the "negative capability" that Keats ascribed to Shakespeare himself.

A few years after I left Prairie, I wrote a poem called "Course Description." It described a course as a beautifully arranged and symmetrical formal garden in which a pack of feral children play tag, kick divots out of the lawn, and trample the flower beds. A reader would not be wrong in detecting here the self-pity of a White Russian émigré grumbling over his third brandy at the Deux Magots. *It was all so perfect until those ignorant workers got in!* Indeed, I had left my most extreme Summerhill phase, but I had not actually reverted to my 1950's boarding school roots. Though written from the position of lost authority, my poem also expresses admiration for the disturbing energy of those wild kids: they keep the garden from becoming a flawless dead space. They make it, as it should and must be, theirs.

Walt Whitman catches the paradox better in "Song of Myself":

> I am the teacher of athletes,
> He that by me spreads a wider breast than my own
>      proves the width of my own
> He most honors my style who learns under it to destroy
>      the teacher.

> I teach straying from me, yet who can stray from me?
> I follow you whoever you are from the present hour;
> My words itch at your ears till you understand them.

Here, giving up authority becomes a way of asserting it more subtly and more effectively: instead of pounding the lectern, we haunt. Whitman is so confident of this legerdemain that his last line strays into *isn't-it-pretty-to-think-so?* territory. Students reluctantly removing their iPod earbuds as they enter the room and stuffing them eagerly back in the moment class is over often seem immune to any itch that I might try to introject. But among the various desperate strategies at our disposal, haunting has a great deal to recommend it. When we haunt, we play neither the stern, domineering father nor the absconded antifather; instead, we get into the grandfather position, where we can be unhurried, a little indulgent, perhaps memorably dotty, and even, with luck and on a good day, something close to wise.

At Prairie as the 1960's lurched toward a close, the grandfather position was unimaginable to me. I seemed only recently to have stopped sucking my own thumb and was fifteen years short of becoming an actual father. Far from having the buffer state of a whole generation between me and the students, I was crammed hard against their borders and often didn't know which side of the line I was supposed to be on. If 30, in one of the famous slogans of the time, marked the point beyond which no one should be trusted, I was still, by a good margin, on *their* side. But the corollary question—whether Jack Mitchell and the other over-30's who ran the school could trust *me*—still had some force in my mind. I despised their Rotarian consciousness (they attended the Club's meetings religiously, bringing back insipid, moralistic slogans to post in the hallways); but a part of me still wanted to please them by becoming the kind of teacher that they thought a teacher should be. Between these divided loyalties I swung, the kind of irresolute liberal that Red Rosa would have remorselessly hunted down.

Listening to the radio one night while scrambling to get together the next day's lessons, I thought I heard Lyndon Johnson say that he had decided not to run for a second term. I had to call a friend to make sure I had not imagined it. I had not, and the confirmation left me oddly disturbed. That a political enemy had fallen could only be good news, but I felt in it a parable that I could not be certain how to read. The authority of authorities had dissolved itself in a breath. Was all authority so vulnerable, so evanescent? Was it a burden to be laid down as soon as possible? If this swaggering blowhard who picked up dogs by the ears and routinely bullied his human subordinates no longer wanted any part of it, what was to be inferred by someone whose ambivalence toward the concept was as pronounced as mine? The questions were pressing, but like all philosophical questions they soon took a back seat to the exigencies of the moment. I had classes to prepare.

# Chapter 7

———✦———

# PATIENCE

ONE OF THE *seedy classrooms at the Cambridge School of Weston, 1980. Raveling carpet, cracked chalkboard, wobbly furniture. My junior writing class, not distinguished by laser-like focus in any case, can't decide where to look. Though the textbooks lie open on the table and we are halfway through a period, Jenny is standing in the door again. Her exits, unilateral and premature—and, even more frustratingly, incomplete—have become a daily feature of the course. She cannot stay seated for more than a few minutes at a time. Regardless of what we may be doing, her anxiety at being here grows almost visibly until it has to play out in motion. Then she stands and starts pacing from corner to corner or hovers in the doorway, uncertain whether to stay or go, a conundrum to herself and a challenge to me, her teacher, who already have more challenges than I want.*

*What to do about Jenny? One line of action would be to say, not unkindly but with a hint of sharpness, "Please come back to the table and sit down—you are distracting us." Tradition sanctions this approach, but Cambridge School does not hold tradition in high regard. One of the early progressive schools and among the first coed boarding schools in the country, it*

*had found itself overtaken in the late 60's when the great establishment acad-*
*emies began to thaw and crack willy-nilly in the heat of the counter-culture.*
*At Andover girls were walking the corridors, boys shucked their coats and*
*ties, and the faculty not only countenanced but actively participated in anti-*
*war moratoria. For CSW, the only way to maintain an identity was to cast*
*aside its old-fashioned genteel liberalism and claim the revolutionary mantle.*
*This it did by making disorganization a point of principle, allowing whim*
*and impulse to run free, and rejecting almost everything (including sitting*
*still at a classroom table) that one naturally thought of when one thought of*
*the word "school." When I arrived in 1977 I had been teaching for 12 years*
*but was still questioning many of these things myself and thought that CSW*
*would be a sympathetic place to do it in. Instead, I soon began to doubt my*
*own vocation and to fear that teaching, which had always seemed so radiant*
*with possibility, was in fact a vain and desperate enterprise.*

*And now, as I feel the attention of the class diffusing, as my own eyes*
*flick back and forth between my book and the girl hesitating in the door-*
*way, I wonder more than ever what I am doing here.*

I knew little about Cambridge School's evolution when I accepted
the job. I was just married; my wife had graduated from CSW some
years earlier and had loved it as a place of culture and serious intellectual life. She remembered great music, exacting science (not her forte),
and literature taught from the heart. Some of the teachers were impressively quirky and many were demanding. Once, she had stayed up all
night to finish a history paper and had asked the teacher if she could
turn the paper in and go back to the dorm and sleep through class. Her
teacher had said no—going to class was an obligation that having pro-
crastinated the paper did not cancel. However tired she was, she had to
be there. This was an answer that Janna could grudgingly respect even
at the time and that she now looked back on as a sign of the school's ex-
cellence. For her, setting up at CSW would be like a homecoming. Her
decade-old memories made it seem like the school I had been looking
for, my perfect match at last.

On the day I came to sign the contract, one of my colleagues-to-be, Chandler, took me for a walk in the woods to set me straight. We shuffled through the pine needles in a little copse behind the boys' dormitory. His tone was conspiratorial, almost as if, even here, he could not be perfectly sure there were no microphones. The school, he said, was a matriarchy. It had fallen into the hands of a circle of women who saw education chiefly as a linear extension of suckling. They had no interest in scholarship or ideas and regarded all discipline as repression. Moreover—and here was the real point to which he wished to alert me—they hated anyone, particularly any man, who challenged their theories, and they had no scruples about politicking with students to destroy the challenger.

I didn't know what to make of Chandler's warning. He was a Boston Brahmin, intelligent and well-spoken, but his evident bitterness and paranoia made me suspicious. I considered myself a feminist and heard more than a little misogyny in his analysis. Though certainly not the whole of education, mothering had in the too-masculine world of my own school days been a conspicuously missing piece. I thought it deserved a place. So I thanked Chandler and decided to keep an open mind. Then I met Regine, the doyenne of the English department and my chief antagonist for the next four years.

Janna, who had to suffer through my alienation from CSW, insists that Regine had her virtues: that she was someone kids genuinely liked and trusted and wanted to talk to. From a distance of 35 years I can just barely see my way to conceding this point and can also acknowledge that even if she had had no virtues at all I should have been able to shrug her off and get on with my business. Back then, though, I found her exactly as Chandler had described her, and she appalled and fascinated me in approximately equal measures. My antipathy, I am uneasy to admit, sprang partly from what is now called "lookism": her loose, baggy smoker's face, immense sack dresses, and bursting carry-alls suggested someone who lived under a bridge or in the back seat of an abandoned car. I dressed casually myself, in the half-hippie, half Maine guide way of the place, but not so casually as to give the impression that I had been sleeping rough for week. If she meant her person as a statement to students, the message seemed to be, "No matter how much you may feel that you are falling apart, I am there with you, falling apart too." This was a form of solidarity that struck me as unhealthy. It demeaned students by assuming that they felt they were breaking down; and if they did feel it, the worst possible response was for an adult to mime joining in the collapse.

Regine's identification with teenagers took many forms. She understood their restlessness because she could not sit still herself. She rarely got through an entire faculty meeting but instead, in the midst of a debate, would gather her widely-strewn belongings and make a noisy exit into the hall. There she would smoke greedily and reflect on her favorite topic, the damage that adult harshness could do to delicate adolescent psyches. She was obsessed with suicide and seemed to believe that the primary, if not the only, mission of a school was to anticipate and prevent it; she had even written a book on the subject. Most of the other teachers at least paid lip service to the idea of limit setting, but Regine regarded rules as at best a distraction and at worst a provocation that might push the fragile over the edge. When we discussed them she either absented herself or simply ignored the agreements we reached. At one meeting the rest of us decided (an unusual show of starch) that, in the interests of at least minimal privacy for the grown-ups, students should no longer be allowed to enter the faculty room. And there she was, the next day, huddled over a typewriter with one of her protégés and plotting the girl's defense in a forthcoming disciplinary hearing, while their cigarettes scorched into the edges of the desktop dark traces of their defiant collusion.

"You're just a bunch of rotten kids," Regine would coo ingratiatingly to a group she found asprawl in the corridor—conveying with well calibrated irony her refusal to accept the cruel categories into which other adults pigeonholed the young and her appreciation of the ineffable beauty and goodness that their louche demeanor could scarcely conceal. (Naturally, their response to this kind of reinforcement was to turn up the dial on louche.) She was so bent on infantilizing others, even—or perhaps especially—colleagues, that she bestowed diminutives on males in positions of what passed for authority at CSW. Jay, the dean of students, became "Jaysie" to her, as if she hoped to divert him into playing with a rattle and forgetting about the command-and-control functions that a dean of students is supposed to perform.

Regine did not produce a baby name for me. Perhaps she found me too forbidding, too unlikely a recruit to her nursery. She did tell me that I was "rigid," the most dreadful pejorative she knew. This label I was willing to accept, since the alternative seemed to be abject limpness, but it hurt a little, too. I had believed I was actually pretty good at nurturing, and now that part of my work was to be denied me so that I could be cast as just another old-school academic hard guy.

It didn't help that I arrived in a year of even more than normal turmoil. At CSW, everyone said, crisis was not just a passing rough patch; crisis was the *curriculum*. The crisis of the moment involved school leadership—whether to find a new head or install the acting head permanently in the position. The acting head, a large, beetle-browed man who responded to pressure by becoming a bully, had somehow won the allegiance of Regine and her claque of libertarians. They didn't like rules, but they could appreciate a fist. The board of trustees—mostly genteel women schooled in more decorous times and places—wanted him gone and seriously underestimated the resistance they were in for. Scenes modeled on the French revolution ensued. Emergency meetings in the dining hall, speeches from table tops. Threats of strikes and mass resignations. Enlistment of brigades of students in the adult business. Eventually a new head was brought in, her position poisoned from the first and her aloof temperament perfectly unsuited for survival in the merciless guerilla war that would follow.

The general tantrum provided fertile ground for a hundred individual tantrums. Kids flew off the handle daily and teachers wrung their hands. Crisis was the curriculum, and what it taught most compellingly was the heady, neurotic pleasure of crisis. Could anything equal the drama of it, the sheer, pulse-pounding sense of self-fulfillment? *I come undone, therefore I exist.* The usual business of school—books to read, writing to do—was tedious in comparison. After some months of this, I started to come undone myself, rubbed raw by the constant fractiousness. Teaching wasn't fun anymore. In the fall of my second year at Cambridge School, I lost my temper at a whining class and stormed out of the room, slamming the door behind me. I took some unscheduled time off, consulted career counselors about the possibility of an entirely new direction. (The test they gave me suggested that I would be good at handling finances for a non-profit.) I read and re-read my favorite passage in the *Iliad*, the one where Akhilleus, insulted by Agamemnon, brandishes the speaker's staff and declares that he has made an irreversible decision to withdraw from the war:

> I swear
> A day will come when every Akhaian soldier
> Will groan to have Akhilleus back. That day
> You shall no more prevail on me than this
> Dry wood shall flourish...

I even sat at the dank counter of a bartenders' school and took the free introductory lesson—hands-on education of the kind Regine favored.

Though no one audibly groaned to have me back, CSW was patient with me. Why not?—I had become its star pupil, a one-time preppy stiff transformed into a studious neophyte in the art of coming undone. At this touching show of human weakness (had I thought I was immune?), the school would fold me to its ample breast. In an odd twist, its patience came easier because it had organized its calendar on the principle of impatience: the Module System! Classes changed every four and a half weeks so that—if students and teachers could endure being together just that long—they could all make for the door at once, getting out before they became sick of each other. "Kids hate having the same teacher all year," Regine said. I thought that a series of transient relationships might not be the best thing either. If you got sick for a week, you missed a quarter of the course; if you didn't want to learn whatever was on offer, you could pretty readily wait for it to go away. Still, when *I* needed to go away for a couple of months, the Module System made it easy enough to replace me temporarily and then to let me slip back in when I came to my senses.

I did come to them, or at least got bored with sulking in my tent. Pouring drinks with cute names and chatting up the barflies did not seem like a tenable alternative either, and I never pursued my diploma in mixology. Instead, on a cold, dark January day, as a new module began, I was there at the head of the table—racked with uncertainty, but there. I wondered if I could survive so much as a single period; the students seemed to be wondering the same thing. But the course was Love in Literature, an almost irresistible theme. After a while, discussion hesitantly began to move. One module followed another, and my crisis—of confidence and, yes, of identity—subsided from a rolling boil to a simmer. I could get through the days, but I still didn't trust my calling. It was hard to distinguish the school's dysfunction from mine. And, two years later, there stood Jenny in the doorway. Would she bolt? Would she take the rest of the class with her? Fidgeting, one foot in and one foot out, she made a living emblem of ambivalence—her own, her classmates', and mine too. If they didn't make a break for it, perhaps I would.

Even in ideal conditions, teaching is a fragile, doubtful enterprise with a high failure rate. "You can't succeed with everyone," a school psychologist once told a seminar of beginning teachers, of whom I was one. At the time, I filed this thought away as the defeatism of the defeated. The failures of my elders were no doubt due to their lack of imagination, their arid personalities, their indifference. Blissfully unmindful that time was a continuum along which I too would travel, I stuffed my shirt with Thoreau's pronouncement that "Age is no better, hardly so well, qualified for an instructor as youth, for it has not profited so much as it has lost." *Not succeed with everyone?—watch me!* was my callow battle cry.

Of course I no sooner started teaching than I began to fail. Students left the room unchanged, arrived at the end of the term no wiser and no more articulate than they had been at the start. I had at least some imagination, my personality tended toward the flamboyant, god knew I was earnest, and anyone could see I was young. (One of my students in the summer of 1966 recently sent me a photo in which I am sitting against an enormous pillar that supports the portico of Andover's main classroom building. Barely visible on my upper lip is the moustache I have grown in order to look just a little more...seasoned. It doesn't work: I am transparently and undeniably young.) With these credentials, what could the problem be?

To help myself resist the temptation to take failures personally, I might have reflected that of the 168 hours in a week a student was spending fewer than four with me. He probably entered these brief encounters with little more than a dull sense of obligation *(It's the next thing on my schedule)*, possibly with active resistance *(Jeez, I wish I didn't have to go to English)*, and almost certainly not with a powerful wish to be transformed *(What?)*. Moreover, the remaining 164-plus hours would offer countless more seductive activities, such as bashing other boys with hockey or lacrosse sticks, listening to very loud music, poring over the latest issue of *Playboy*, or, if possible, canoodling in the bushes with real girls. Even sleeping—what teenager ever gets enough of it?—would claim a higher spot on the pleasure ladder than intellectual exertion.

I did not reflect any of these things, in part because I had been that rare anomaly, an intellectual teenager. One of my boarding school roommates, assigned to do an early-morning bird count as a field biology project, quite sensibly slept in and made up what he hoped were plausible numbers; I often woke myself at 5:30 to read, with almost sensual delight, whatever novel Emory Basford had given us that week. I did not much like loud music and had taken the separation of the sexes at school as a comfortable given. Thus, I was badly placed to understand the strength of the current against which I or any teacher would have to swim. It took me a long time to see that most students were less like me than I at first imagined and even longer to begin figuring out what to do about their stubborn insistence on being themselves.

Moreover, in my own first years of teaching, I was scarcely aware of my failures. Just keeping my head above water required nearly all my attention and energy and kept me from noticing that I was being swept backward. And the heroic narrative that I had constructed from images of my own best teachers, like Basford and Royce, blurred my sense of what was actually going on around me. Easier to imagine myself as the charismatic or revered figure in the center than to probe too deeply into possible misapprehensions on the periphery. Anyway, I was in a business that had no bottom line. The tests and the papers looked at first glance like accountability but turned out to be a mere illusory scrim over learning that might or might not be taking place underneath. The real results, intangible in any case, might be delayed so long that the students were out of school and well advanced in their lives before they became aware, if they ever did, that they had been changed—if they had.

This facile excuse for accomplishing nothing was also a real, inescapable, and tormenting fact of a teacher's life. You didn't know and probably never would know what you taught. I dimly realized this even as I started out, and everything since has confirmed it. Sometimes tantalizing clues arrive even decades later. The phone rings and it is Suzanne, who left my school abruptly for another one but who remembers just what happened in that class on Shakespeare and wants to discuss her own child's education. An alumni bulletin comes in the mail, and in it is a long note from Andy, whom I felt I treated with testiness bordering on cruelty but who now credits me with having given direction to his feckless and amorphous teenage days. These messages are like signals from deep space, the crackling, barely audible transmissions of a probe lost among the stars. More mundane and more predictable is the feeling that descends regularly every June as the last strains of commencement music die away. Then I suffer a sudden hollowness, a lack of faith in what I have been doing. Those classes that seemed so full of life, those relationships that seemed so meaningful are touched at once by a withering wand, become ghosts in a dusty attic. I don't know what I've taught, and I probably never will. The only thing to do is wait and hope for a sign. Patience, patience.

In my first spring at Milton Academy, where I came after parting ways with Cambridge School, I stopped by the baseball diamond on a May afternoon to watch the team play its arch rival in the final game of the season. The coach was my new department chair, Guy Hughes, and he had a strong team that year, led by a lefthanded pitcher who was overwhelming when zeroed in but who, like many lefties, occasionally suffered bouts of wildness. In the last inning, with Milton narrowly ahead, the wildness set in and the pitcher loaded the bases on walks. As the recipient of the third free pass jogged down to first, I saw Guy rise slowly from the bench and begin to make his way to the mound. He was a good athlete himself and a frequent squash player, but now he moved like a man recovering from a double hip replacement. He seemed to take a full minute to reach the foul line, another minute to join his struggling pitcher on the hill. Once there, he spoke a quiet sentence or two, then made his way back at the same pace to the bench. Something about these deliberate movements drained the angst and tension out of the moment. I realized that I had seen an extraordinary display of patience, visible teaching of a high order. The pitcher retired the side.

Patience was something I had never had enough of myself. Perhaps I reacted early against my patient dad's glacial passage through life. I was grateful that he untangled my backlashes, but he drove all of us crazy with his refusal to move until the planets were perfectly aligned. An expert photographer, he once undertook to teach my sister how to use one of his sophisticated cameras, but when he had not yet let her touch it by the end of a full day's tutorial, her interest waned. I rushed things, tried to force them when they didn't go the first time, tended to swear at them and abandon them after the second or third. This approach, honed on model airplanes that didn't fit together, lawn mowers that wouldn't start, and tennis strokes that wound up over the baseline or in the net, extended naturally to students who wouldn't behave or wouldn't learn.

Older people gave me a lot of rope as I flopped around trying to figure out what I was doing as a teacher. Perhaps they should have been less patient or should have tried in a formal way to introduce me to the basics of the craft, though I probably would have resented it and thought I knew better. The style in those days did not favor training or mentoring. You just got in there and learned on the fly. My first headmaster, Jack Mitchell at Prairie, certainly regretted that he had hired me, especially after he repeated the mistake by hiring a second Ivy League know-it-all the following year. He liked the Ivy League part but wasn't so keen on the rest of the package. We mocked him mercilessly and mocked the school's pious and conventional culture. Meanwhile, my teaching was as erratic as any southpaw's deliveries. I won over the smart kids without any trouble and favored them shamelessly but didn't have a clue what to do with the dull-witted or recalcitrant—with Paul, who muttered mutinous asides; with Tom, who clowned non-stop; with Anne Marie, who just didn't have a clue (and was so dysgraphic that she couldn't even get the left-hand margin of a page to line up). There were many more of these. My capricious disciplinary approach was worse than useless. Jack knew all this but still didn't fire me. When I left under my own power after three years, he wrote me a kind thank-you letter. It was in the turgid and fulsome style of all his communications, but the kindness broke through; and I was aware, even as I groaned at the phraseology, that he had generously let me get away with one.

I should have learned from Jack's example that generosity toward those who are works in progress, even if they do not seem to be working hard enough and their progress appears all but imperceptible, is the right way to go. We are all works in progress and will be sure to need the favor returned. In fact, my best impulses were compassionate, but I often found myself too threatened by insubordination to take the humane way. I clamped down when I could have let the resistance vent itself harmlessly. Much of the time I could not be patient even with myself.

If a frustrating reality of teaching is that you don't know and may never know your results (even the canner at the sardine factory gets to count the cans at the end of the day!), the happier flip side is that the book is never closed. As a culture, we are enamored of redemption stories, many of them bogus. Nevertheless, when you teach, every failure is a redemption waiting to happen, and this prospect, realized or not, is one of the things that make the work possible. In the past 25 years or so, I've tried to create more chances for redemption by organizing assignments into long-term projects, with time for false starts, midcourse corrections, and last-minute saves. The memoir writing project that I do with seniors goes on for three months and even has a two-week vacation in the middle of it for those who need a serious chance to breathe and regroup, as many do. Michael, for one, decided to scrap his first draft completely and write about something different. He was right—the draft, flimsy and superficial, was headed nowhere—but he couldn't get going on the new idea, couldn't even say with any assurance what the new idea was. Looking over his shoulder at the blank screen, my anxiety mounted. Even a skillful and disciplined writer like him could not climb out of the hole he was digging. With a weekend to go, he had next to nothing. Then, on Monday, he handed me the fully developed and expertly finished story of his friendship with the maintenance man's son at summer camp—the best thing I have ever seen a student write about social class.

Examples multiply. Roy, a sullen, resentful boy and a weak writer, turns in a childish cartoon of a first draft about a typhoon-swept kayaking expedition in the South China Sea—all sound and fury, signifying little. I tell him that non-stop action doesn't work, that he needs to characterize his friends, reflect on what happened, and find a center. The truth is that I don't expect much; nothing I have seen in him suggests that he has the mental elasticity and sophistication to improve this piece, or the will. Yet when I read the final, especially a scene where, in a flapping tent on a tiny island, he and his schoolmates huddle naked and terrified while the wind howls around them, I find myself thinking about *King Lear*. Somewhere in himself, Roy has discovered the resources to give his story powerful shape.

Then there is Dana, who has worked hard on a memoir about her struggles with eating, has pressed herself courageously down through the surface layers to the core of the experience, has done everything right. What she still lacks on the last day is a conclusion worthy of the rest. She tries this and that, knows each time that it doesn't work. One ending is too neat, another too aimless, a third too sentimental. I keep nudging her, with one eye on the clock. No matter how long a project is, time eventually must run out. Finally, five minutes before she has to press the print button, she strikes an image of a piece of rum cake that her mother made for her and that tasted—and was the first thing in months that had tasted—unambiguously good. Brava! The moment rings with all the ambiguity as well as the release. It is a perfect way to end the piece, and finding it is a perfect way to end the project. The printer whirs obligingly to life.

Patience rewarded? Perhaps so, but even such black-and-white successes must be classed in the tentative category. After momentary elation when I praise his memoir to the skies (overlooking the many passages of clumsy and incorrect writing that it still contains), Roy reverts to sullenness. His course evaluation later reveals that he thinks I have graded him harshly all year and also been insensitive to cultural differences that surfaced in his work. Who do I think I am to question him, he wants to know. Dana and several of her classmates, who have been unusually sweet with one another since September, cry on the last day of school. I cry a little too, touched by how deeply they are touched. Kids cry when they leave the dormitories, where they've lived like families for three or four years, but ordinarily not at the end of a course, where the formalities of academic life keep emotion tamped down. This group is different. Tears flow, hugs are exchanged, it has all meant something to them. A week later they graduate and are gone. Years pass, and I hear next to nothing from or about them. Has Dana kept finding perfect images? Is she able to find them because I nudged her not to give up on that first one? What about her classmates, many of whom had their own breakthroughs that year? Do they remember success and build on it? Do they remember me? I wait for distant signals. The first round of patience is as nothing beside the long second round.

I teach; therefore, I wait. This old man's axiom would have seemed far too passive in my early days, when I wanted to leap at everything and seize it by the throat. Sometimes it still seems like a rationalization for letting things slide. After students have gone off to begin their adult lives, waiting becomes your only option, but while they are in front of you, grab them and shake them hard. If you wander too far in the name of patience, you may cross the shadowy border into indifference.

Well, even indifference has its self-protective uses. Reason says that you will lose many of the battles you choose to fight and that, to improve your odds, you should choose the fight-worthy battles carefully and concede the rest. Nothing can be gained from badgering Roy about comma splices when he has impregnably fortified himself against the very idea of learning from you. Beat against the walls as you like, you may have no recourse but to hope that he will find another teacher later, when he is ready for one. In the meantime, though you are chosen to shoulder some responsibility for him, you must set a limit on how much of it you will accept. The idea that all failures are the teacher's, currently a fashionable bromide in education, is as nonsensical as its antithesis in hickory-stick days, the idea that all failures are the student's. Even if you have a clearer image of the ideal shape than I can honestly claim, how far, in your paltry four hours a week, can you bend the product of stubborn nature and haphazard nurture?

Students are often busy battling themselves, and the furor of the clash pushes you to the sidelines, as irrelevant as the ladies and gentlemen who rode down in carriages from Washington to watch Bull Run and then had to whip up the horses and flee for their lives when the cannon balls started coming too close. I have learned to cherish strugglers, to seize any small chances I may have to lean in on the good guys' side, and, above all, not to mind the stray shots that sometimes whistle around my ears. It becomes a point of honor to stay with someone who doesn't understand why he is thrashing destructively about and who probably doesn't like it any better than I do.

My honor wavered a couple of years ago when Chloe returned from an eight-month suspension and showed up on one of my class lists. I didn't want to teach her. She had been busted for hacking into the school's computer records and changing some grades. The changes were not egregious—a plus here, a minus there—and the episode seemed as much a mischievous experiment as a crime. But grades are currency (even if an inflatable one), and no school can let them be counterfeited or tampered with; from that point of view she was lucky not to be expelled outright, as she certainly would have been if the boys in the back room at Andover in the old days had gotten hold of her. Myself, I wouldn't have minded the disciplinary record so much, but she was also said to be hell in the classroom. One colleague railed that, as a sophomore, she had virtually destroyed his course with her self-centeredness. Because I knew that railing was his way and that he must have found it especially hard to have a second self-centered person in the room, I discounted everything he said by about 50%. Still, it was enough to send me to the scheduling office to see if I could get her moved. I rationalized that she had begun my course with another teacher the year before and had completed a month of it before being suspended; it would be redundant for her.

The schedule was locked in, I found, and any change would result in a long domino-cascade of further changes—more trouble than I could in conscience ask my friends in the office to take. And conscience, now that it had awakened, brought a message that cut deeper still: I should not have gone to the office in the first place, because doing so violated one of my first principles: you have to teach those who fall to your lot.

Chloe had fallen to mine, and she delighted me from the first. Perhaps her previous courses had been like keys that scratched plaintively around the lock but never found the slot. Perhaps the suspension had actually done what suspensions are intended for but often fail in: made her reflect. She knew she was skating on thin ice, certainly; but, better, she had the energy of a fresh start and a little more self-knowledge. I was surprised to find, given what I had heard about her, that her keynote was not self-centeredness but generosity. She was an excellent writer, probably the best in the class, but she seemed at least as interested in her classmates' writing as in her own. When we discussed work in progress, she always put extra time into thinking about the other kids' pieces; she offered smart, useful advice, and she expressed it so gently and encouragingly that the writer could hear and use it. Everyone benefited from her being there.

Though she never required so much as a grain of patience from me, Chloe must have finally expended her own in the effort of being good. A week before graduation she sold the school bookstore some used textbooks that she had found in a common room and were not hers to sell. Her prior record worked against her. She had not graduated with her first senior class and now would not be allowed to graduate with her second, either. My railing colleague found tasty satisfaction in this denouement: it was proof that we should never have taken her back at all. He may have been right—a school that lacks edges *does* lack a center, and the ax that administrators wielded so blithely in the 50's to punish the moral equivalent of stealing a crust of bread can never become a mere historical relic in any conceivable utopian future. Chloe had used up her chances. Nevertheless, if there had been any possibility of offering her a third senior year, I would have voted for it.

At Cambridge School in 1980, Jenny paced the perimeter ready to bolt, and I wondered once again whether I might as well tend bar as teach. The suspense of watching her try to make up her mind wore me out. I had one eye only for her and one for all the rest, an unfair distribution; but something (could it have been Regine's nicotine-edged voice whispering in my ear?) told me that to order her back to the table—to try to break her—would be, even if it succeeded superficially, a fruitless exercise of power. The stalemate went on. Eventually, I found a way to send them all out of the room. They were to go into Boston and develop a piece based on observation and reporting. The assignment might raise a new set of anxieties in wavering Jenny, but at least my own stomach wouldn't have to churn with them minute by minute.

A few days later she came back and laid her paper on my desk. Reading it, I quickly saw that she had channeled every bit of her energy, both the urge to flee and the contrary struggle to restrain herself, into the work of seeing and writing. She had an exquisite sensibility and her language buzzed and snapped. I read the piece a second time. It was better than I could have written, and it was worth waiting for.

# Chapter 8

***

# TIME

ONE AFTERNOON AT *Milton I am sitting alone at my classroom table, reading papers and rather enjoying the solitude. Convoluted as the problems that a student essay presents may be, you can take them one at a time; they pose, if not a relief, at least an agreeable variation from the whirlwind of agendas that compete for attention during a class.*

*I've had a normally gusty day. This morning, three of my four classes went well enough, but the seventh-grade boys, with a group of prospective students visiting, launched a series of shenanigans that completely subverted my plans for the period. After the visitors had left, I chided the class—rather lightly, I thought. No great damage had been done. The subversion of plans to some extent is a daily occurrence in middle school teaching, and who could say that the merry-making had not actually been an attraction to the guests, happy perhaps to imagine themselves attending a school that was not in perpetual lockdown mode. I was peeved, but not seriously so, and I chided pro forma and thought little about it.*

*Now, however, as I sit here with my papers, the door opens and Gary enters—handsome, charismatic Gary, who often leads the class to its successes but who was also a ringleader in the morning's disruptions. He stands there looking stricken for several seconds without saying anything. Then, instead of words, tears begin to flow. They keep on flowing as he finds his voice to apologize for behaving so badly. Stricken myself by the depth of his remorse, I keep trying to interrupt him to say that the behavior had not been so* very *bad. But there is no staying this powerful surge of conscience—conscience that no doubt is securely grounded in the way Gary's parents have raised him but that now finds strong, independent expression in an encounter with the world. In the morning, he had been a cub playing with other cubs; in the afternoon, he is taking a step back to reflect, a step back that is a step forward along the arc of his life.*

So many intersecting arcs in the geometry of being a teacher. Each student must be tracked along his own unevenly ascending curve, and the observation—a problem in relativity—is complicated by the teacher's perhaps equally uncertain place on the trajectory of his career. We must be alert to where we are in the cycle of a school year and in the narrative arc of the book we are teaching. And always there is the granular flow of daily time, begging us to manage it and mischievously slipping away.

My first classes in the fall of 1965 may have meant little to the sophomores who sat in them, but they taught me lessons both in the intractable nature of time and in the law of diminishing returns. I had been assigned two sections of the same course, the generic English 2 in the plodding curriculum of the day. This was English *qua* English— some grammar, some writing, some literature, no big ideas, and seemingly no heavy lifting for even a recent college graduate just starting out. Still, I quickly found myself pressed for time.

A single preparation should not take more than an hour; having only a single one to worry about, I watched helplessly as it expanded through the watches of the evening. Some of that time did burn up in aimless worry—the worry that still, after decades, clings to almost every class, making me hesitate and draw a deep breath before I close the door to begin: *Will things go well?* Most of it, however, went into an earnest and reasonably well-focused effort to line up my ducks for the next day. I would spend two hours, maybe three, laying out everything that needed to be said about Stephen Crane's "The Open Boat." Then in the morning I would go in and squander my ammunition in 12 minutes, with 38 left to go and no help in sight. My own talk never lasted as long as I thought it would, and because it sounded discouragingly hollow in my ears I often let it peter out even before the stuff from my notes was exhausted. I understood that one was supposed to ask questions, and I did; but I couldn't figure out how to ask a question that was not a dead end. My questions all had answers. The answers ranged from a word to a sentence—tops!—and did not lead to further questions. Class advanced in a series of sticky jerks and long, fruitless silences. At the end of the period, if we got that far, the boys' sense of relief was palpable but fell far short of mine.

What I did not understand then and did not fully grasp for a long time is that teaching is not about filling empty space: it is about creating an empty space for others to fill. This should be far simpler than what God did when he created the heavens and the earth. He took a void and introduced wonderfully elaborate matter; all we need to do is manufacture the right kind of void.

That it's not so simple comes as no surprise when we consider all the mediocre and downright bad teaching that we had when we were growing up. Much of it was done by honorable people who saw void-filling as their essential task and plied the pump handles dutifully. Some of it was done by those who recognized that there was a better way but couldn't quite get it to work. As Didi points out to Gogo in *Waiting for Godot*, "There's no lack of void." It comes in all shapes and sizes, from demitasse to universal gulp. And it tends to be dark and scary, the imagined abode of spiders, the inhospitable wasteland between the stars. What we need is a space that beckons and invites, a homey void.

Eventually, I learned some things that help. People are more willing

BE A TEACHER

to enter a space where they are recognized, so it helps to learn every kid's name by the second day and to use the names constantly. I greet students one by one as they trickle in. Good morning, Caleb. Subtext: I notice that you're here and I'm glad to see you; I hope you're also reasonably glad to see me. Warming up the room this way not only feels good but has the effect of a performative—an utterance that brings about its own fulfillment. Performatives have all kinds of uses in teaching. Tell someone that she has good insights and she may well start looking more deeply into things. Tell someone that you are glad to see him and you are more likely to *be* glad—if only because his natural response will be to make himself more likable. Welcome, Caleb. Thanks for sharing this void with me.

Once everyone has arrived and been saluted as a presence, the process of shaping the space to receive intellectual content begins. Nature abhors a vacuum, and any old thing may rush in to fill this one—the latest gossip from the Student Center, replays of the hilarious skit in this morning's assembly, assessment of the likelihood that this afternoon's game will be rained out. Deft is the teacher who can seize on one of these rogue incursions and redirect it to the matter at hand—and manage the rerouting so gently that the conversation seems to migrate of its own accord. One minute we are talking about Bobby's fender-bender on the way to school, the next minute about *Romeo and Juliet*.

A particularly gentle way of starting is to ask everyone to write for five minutes, maybe ten, about some question from the reading the class did last night. This is low-stakes writing, writing that I am never going to grade or even look at. As the students write, the silence is a kind of unspoken performative: it calms them and focuses them. In contrast to discussion, where the chances are all too good that only one person will think at a time, low-stakes writing requires everyone to think at once. I do mine right along with the class and am still sometimes surprised at how effectively it prepares me for talking; things I noticed vaguely when I did the reading sharpen into expressible points. The same crystallization takes place in students' heads. When the talking does start, everyone has something to say; and everyone goes home with a written record of his own thinking, perhaps embroidered with notes about what others thought.

The key to low-stakes writing is to ask the right question. *A* right question, anyway—or maybe two or three, so that there is plenty to talk about. The key to asking a right question is that it be real. To qualify as real, it must be difficult to answer, open to points of view, evocative of debate. If Milton loves God so much, why does he give Satan all the good lines? If Thoreau thinks that people cannot learn from one another, does he have any business writing a book? If your classmate wants to improve this draft, what are some strategies that she should consider? When a colleague of mine retired recently, another colleague eulogized her by recalling how her constant refrain in class was, "Yes, but what is the *question?*" She was pushing the process a necessary step farther, asking students to frame their own uncertainties. The most interesting parts of literature are those that disturb and unsettle us, perplex us with contradictions, make us scramble for our footing. As soon as I can—as soon as I have modeled what a real question is—I want students to do the asking that sets us in motion every day.

"Like a piece of ice on a hot stove," Robert Frost wrote, "a poem rides on its own melting." The progress of the ice depends on what it releases as it goes; in the case of writing a poem, you don't know where line 12 will take you until line 11 has deliquesced out of line 10. Classes, too—and whole courses—should ride like ice on a stove. Their speed and direction should be unpredictable, and the teacher should not be poking and nudging them all the time in order to make them follow his preconceived route. If he supplies the genial warmth in the firebox, the melting will take place without his intervention and friction will drop to zero. One question will lead to another, responses will evoke counter-responses. The tiniest tilt in the stove's surface will be the hill down which the whole experience happily slides. At last the teacher will glance at the clock or the calendar and realize that the time to stop has sneaked up on him, and instead of feeling relieved he will regret having to interrupt such natural and graceful motion. Even the students, though perhaps few of them would admit it, may be sorry to leave the room.

Of course this utopian picture often does not correspond to reality. How could it in a world as cluttered with cross-purposes as a school? Kids carry their own agendas, and no matter how effusively I greet them they may not be in the right frame of mind to ride the hot stove with me. Their moods can last for an hour or a week, can turn on a dime or linger through an entire year—part of a phase of development in which they are completely inaccessible to me. And their moods, for better and for worse, can be contagious. I think of Ray—ironic name!—whose morose features and aura of condescension projected such intense gloom into every corner of the room that his classmates soon sank into mute and abject despair. Eventually, so did I. An intelligent and capable guy, Ray, the best writer in the class—and he brooded over it like doom. Perhaps the year before he had been the life of the party; perhaps the next year he was again dancing with a lampshade on his head. My year: darkness visible.

I can't claim that my own moods are always helpful, either. Take a grey winter morning. Multiply it by the arrival of a large, unexpected bill. Multiply it again by the discovery that the sump pump has given up and there are six inches of water in the basement. A severe case of seasonal affective disorder is my baseline, and when circumstances pile on I often do not do an effective job of stoking the stove. On days like that, I am looking for the anti-Ray, someone who can humor me back to life or at least engage me in humoring him. Surprisingly often, a student will step forward to play that part, arriving with a little jolt of energy or in a state of teaseable dishevelment.

Even if my mood is exuberant, I may not make the right moves. A good-enough class is not too hard to achieve, especially if you've established momentum in the weeks and months before it. The school year is like a rocket-launch, with 95% of the fuel expended in the first minute or two of flight; after that, you can mostly glide. But a *great* class requires, in addition to momentum and a dash of luck, some delicate intuitive tweaks. True, you mustn't be prodding things to move against their natural direction, but you *are* the pilot and you have to steer and your choices make a big difference. You can ruin it all by letting someone go on too long or by cutting her off too abruptly, by demanding too much precision or by tolerating too much vagueness, by discouraging a worthwhile digression or permitting the pack to bay down a false trail in hopes that it may lead to something. You can ruin it by looking a speaker too insistently in the eye, so that he locks in on you and forgets that there are a dozen other people in the room that he should also be talking to. You can ruin it by poking your nose into uncomfortable silences before they have had a chance to ripen or by letting them linger until silence itself becomes the only topic on any-one's mind. Even the angle of your torso can be decisive. Lean in and you assert a commanding presence that might seem teacherly to the headmaster if he happens to be visiting that day but that is also likely to nudge the class into a posture of passivity. Lean back and you open that homey, inviting space for their energies to fill, but unless you have shaped it carefully they may fill it with stuff that is little better than more void. Or, worse, they may interpret your artful self-effacement as indifference and decide to go limp themselves.

There are so many ways to go wrong, and overshadowing the whole experience is the finite and unrepeatable nature of time. We won't get that class back, and we can't count on a lot more chances to make it right, either. Like anything in short supply, time becomes an obsession for teachers. We are jealously alert to get our share, fixing the evil eye on students who wander in late and resenting the well-intentioned schedule rearrangements of administrators who think they are serving a higher educational purpose but in fact are just cutting into our class time. Once, at Prairie School, Jack Mitchell caved in to a trustee who was a doctor. He loaded everyone in the upper school onto buses for a two-hour trek to an event called the Wisconsin Work Week of Health. We weren't actually to spend a week there—only a day of lectures on hygiene and such. But a day proved too long and a large contingent of students managed to slip away and throw a party for themselves upstairs in one of the rooms of the hotel where the Work Week was being held. Next morning, as Jack thundered out the requisite self-righteous scolding to the school, I self-righteously reflected that he had brought the outrage on himself by sponsoring the boondoggle in the first place. I, 24 years old and scarcely able to figure out how to keep a class smoldering fitfully for a full period, nevertheless felt a profound indignation at having the time taken from me.

The wish to hold on to the time we are given is matched by the equally futile wish that we could be given more. Departments jockey for position, hoping to gain a few extra minutes at each other's expense. Whole wars may be fought (academic wars: so vicious because the stakes are so small), but in the end the borders remain about as they were and the sum of the time that students spend in school is just the same. Occasionally there are movements for lengthening the school year. We are warned that our calendar still reflects the agrarian rhythms of the 19th century. If we keep taking time out from school to harvest the potatoes, the Chinese will eat our lunch. Fortunately, despite all the hand-wringing, these movements do not succeed. Agrarian rhythms don't look so bad once we start considering the industrial rhythms that presumably would replace them. True, we no longer need our teenagers to bring in the crops, but our teenagers still need time to loaf and invite their souls. The law of diminishing returns again. We could run an 11-month school year and get less done than we now do in nine.

When the recurrent fantasies about expanding time die down, we often replace them with fantasies about the benefits of restructuring the time we have. The 45-minute block becomes the whipping boy for everything that is not going as we would like it to. What we could accomplish if only we had longer blocks! It is hard to remember at these dreamy moments that if we had longer blocks we would have fewer of them and they would arrive less often—that whatever we might gain in continuity of vertical time, we would lose in continuity of horizontal time.

I entered the utopia of the long block when I came to teach at the Cambridge School in 1977. Courses met for two 90-minute periods a day and lasted for four-and-a-half weeks. A student would have four-and-a-half weeks of full-time English, then four-and-a-half weeks of Math, then four-and-a-half weeks of Art; seven of these units made up a school year. This was the Module System, which had been devised in the early 70's as part of a marketing strategy to return Cambridge School to the vanguard of progressivism, a position from which the nationwide educational experiments of the previous decade had dislodged it. Before the Module System, the school had flavored its fundamentally traditional approach with just a soupçon of John Dewey. But the blend had become as musty as the physical plant; the balance sheet had grown redder. Then it occurred to someone that Cambridge School had no less time at its disposal than any other school and that repackaging it and selling the new package as an educational revolution was the way to get back in the black.

In fact, the new container did have advantages. For one thing, it eliminated the static from other courses. No one could come in and claim that he hadn't read the story for English because he had had to prepare for a big math test that day. The math teachers would get their chance next month; for now, you owned the territory, and there was a lot of it. You could pack up and take the kids on a field trip to Walden Pond without compromising someone else's program. You could make them roll up their sleeves and plunge to the elbows in clay; they'd have time to throw the piece, get it in the kiln, and clean up the studio before the day was over. "Hands-on" was the watchword of the Module System. If you want to know the taste of a pear, you must change the pear by eating it yourself—so said Chairman Mao, and he had a point.

Nevertheless, there is a limit to how many pears one can eat at a sitting. Ninety minutes lasts a long time in the life of a 16-year-old. I remember teaching a class on the second floor of the CSW academic building and day after day hearing the staircase rumble with the feet of students whose class on the floor above had run out of gas and been dismissed 20 minutes early. The proponents of the system insisted that teachers had to *learn* to use the longer blocks and that the key was to break up your activities so that you weren't doing the same thing the whole time. This made sense but led to an awkward question: if you have to reset in the middle anyway, why not have two periods of half the length and, in the interim, give students a chance to accrue something that they can bring back to the group?

At its best, the Module System created a space in which a student could focus all her energies on a single project with an imaginable time-frame. Most of us, even teenagers, can think and plan a month in advance; seeing the finish line from the start encourages us to run. Unfortunately, not all learning can be organized into project form; much of it proceeds in small increments rather than heroic leaps. Students need time—horizontal time—to repeat, reflect, and assimilate. Teachers need to reiterate in February, and then again in May, what they said in September. In practice, the short track of a module too often encouraged kids *not* to run—to wait it out and get on to something different. They knew they could outlast you, because in February and May you would no longer be there to remind them of that September point. And even those who worked hard all the way faced months and months of exile from the subject as the modules rolled around. The foreign language teachers tore their hair out. Four-and-a-half weeks of French, and then *rien*—the long forgetting. Learning to write English didn't go so well, either. Some pears need to be savored slowly and at length.

The Module System was a religion at Cambridge School, and the zeal of its true believers evoked my oppositional tendencies, making it hard for me to recognize its strong points. I was thrilled, when I came to Milton Academy, to get back into a schedule in which all courses ran for an entire year and met for 45 minutes four days a week. It didn't feel like the same old thing; it felt like sanity restored. And to me it still makes sense as a way to distribute the time we have. However we decide to carve up and parcel out that time, we will certainly be frustrated by the constraints of our chosen system. What we should remember—the salve for all that inevitable chafing—is that, in the end, time is on our side.

Time is on our side because, as it passes, people change and grow. They grow regardless of our efforts to help them and regardless of the mistakes that we make in those efforts. Often they grow without being aware of it themselves. The growth can be quick and dramatic, as Gary's attack of conscience seemed to be, or slow and barely visible. Most often, people grow in tiny increments, with months and years separating the closely-spaced pencil marks on the doorjamb. Only time-lapse photography can capture the stages of such deliberate blossoming. This is why I have always liked teaching someone a second and even a third time, encountering him once perhaps in seventh grade, again in ninth, and finally when he is a senior. Then I can track, in a way that would not be possible in the tight frame of a single school year, the unfolding of the petals; and the second time is almost always better than the first, the third than the second.

Sometimes these three-act plays can be redemption stories with complicated plotlines of progress and relapse. Elaine was such a pest in my Lower School chess program that after months of struggle I finally had to ask her to leave so that I could get something done with the other kids. When she showed up in my sophomore English class, I was worried about a rerun, but she settled right in, worked hard, and was a sardonically funny contributor to our conversations. In the last paragraph of the last essay of the year, however, she used a word—"anomie"—that I knew very well could not be in her vocabulary. Wearily and reluctantly, I traced the sentence on the Internet and found that she had lifted large chunks of her essay on *The Skin of Our*

*Teeth* from a newspaper review of the play. Confrontation and tears followed—this time, I thought, tears not so much of pure contrition as of misery at being caught and punished.

Elaine's plagiarism earned her a five-day suspension and she had to miss her team's climactic lacrosse game. It would have been a lousy way to end the year, but the year in fact was not quite over: the class was to perform a scene from *The Crucible* in which I had cast Elaine in the key part of the malevolent Abigail. She had not been able to practice with the group while suspended, but after she returned we squeezed in a last rehearsal and hoped for the best—that she could channel her own anger and confusion into the character. In the event she did well, screaming imaginary demons down from the rafters and stamping her feet in highly plausible indignation. She could easily have sunk the show in pique at having been busted but chose instead to go all in. I thanked her for her generosity, figuring that we had brought things to a reasonable finish and that I would not be seeing her again. As a senior, however, she came back for more, signing up for an elective I was teaching on *Hamlet*. It was not a course she had to take and not one I thought was in her wheelhouse. Half of her apparently felt the same way, as she flirted with dropping it but eventually stayed in and, as a final project, joined classmates in making a hilarious video parody of Ophelia's encounter with Hamlet in the nunnery scene. True to her own character if not to the text, she played the part as a spitfire, flipping her hair indignantly, yanking from its socket the plug of the TV on which Hamlet is watching cartoons, balling up his love letters and throwing them in his face. It was a *tour de force*.

Did Elaine persevere because she felt that she still owed me something for her "anomie" scam of two years before? She could never have said so, because her conscience, unlike Gary's, was deep below the surface. But I like to think of her as a struggler for redemption.

Kids who struggle, with me and with themselves, have a special appeal. They engage my compassion and get my adrenaline flowing. I would rather reach a tentative standoff with a struggler than admire the smooth curve of someone else's untroubled ascent toward maturity. Where I teach, there are plenty of dependable students who gradually attain mastery and, when they graduate, are well on their way to being fully realized people. Working with them is a constant satisfaction. It entertains me, exhilarates me, and, in the end, gives me a sense of accomplishment. But it is largely a matter of standing back and letting time, which is on my side, do its thing. With the strugglers nothing can be taken for granted. My work matters more. Here, near the end of life, I must wade back into the turbulent waters of adolescence without being sure where the current is taking us.

# Chapter 9

---

# BOOKS

*OLIVIA AND LIZZIE on a Friday morning. The wick end of the school week, it is a time for us to get on our feet and try to regenerate some of the energy that the exertions of the previous four days have drained away. I have even sometimes resorted to a session of jumping jacks and deep knee bends, but these are seniors and too grown up for a strategy that might snap a class of freshmen out of its daze. Besides, the course is Shakespeare, and the material itself provides a perfect opportunity for what Rousseau long ago identified as the basis of successful educational plans: replacing talk with action.*

*When I first taught the plays, I thought that paraphrase and précis were going to be my most useful tools. Far more useful, it turns out, is simply reading aloud, perhaps preceded by a silent reading, perhaps not. Shakespeare's language is surprisingly impervious to our failure to understand it syllable-by-syllable. It has an uncanny ability to generate meaning that is more than the sum of its parts. If students can enter boldly into the dramatic situation, they can surf along the back of the text for a long, thrilling ride that doesn't depend on counting molecules of water and salt.*

*Olivia is particularly good at this. She can take a passage she has never seen before and clothe it in all the right tones even as she stumbles over some of the words. If I ask her to do it standing up, she can supply the body language, too. This morning she and Lizzie have taken full advantage of the ten minutes I gave them to work out a scene between Mercutio and Benvolio. Olivia, ordinarily a bit of a fashion plate with a strong sense of feminine style, is suddenly all feisty male energy and bravado. Why is Benvolio so annoyingly calm and agreeable? Doesn't he see that a good fight with those cocky Capulets is in the offing? Olivia shadow-boxes rings around her partner, delivers a nuggie to his too-placid shoulder, lashes him with macho sarcasm. I think she is—at nine o'clock on an impromptu Friday morning, no less—the best Mercutio I have ever seen. Probably, being a proficient academician, she could write an acceptable paraphrase, too, but where would be the joy in that? Where, both for her and her audience of laughing classmates, would be the Shakespeare?*

Olivia seized a book and possessed it the way we wish, wistfully, that all students would possess the books we give them. She breathed it, inhabited it, embodied it. Words on a page became lived experience. In this case, of course, the experience, had she lived it out all the way, was destined to end unhappily, with four dead teenagers and two miserable families. If we really do want students to enter their reading in the flesh, perhaps we should be more careful about what we ask them to read? A movement is currently afoot on college campuses that would require professors to put something like a surgeon-general's warning on works that students might find disturbing. Do its advocates have a case?

Headmaster and gadfly Donald Barr once published an opinion piece in the New York *Times* under the title "Should Holden Caulfield Read These Books?" The books in question were *A Separate Peace, To Kill a Mockingbird, Lord of the Flies*, and, of course, *The Catcher in the Rye*. "Holden Caulfield" was understood to be the average high school student. The answer was no.

Barr argued well, jolting me, who had happily taught all four of the novels, first into resistance and then into reconsideration. His position, which he qualified in the case of the relatively benign *Mockingbird*, was that adolescents need positive images of adulthood so that they can grow up to become productive adults. Why, he asked, unless we want to subvert our most basic purpose as teachers, would we choose to present students with remorselessly negative pictures of the world? Why show them a friendship so riddled with jealousy that it can hardly be distinguished from war? Why show them children lapsing into murderous savagery within days of their arrival on a seemingly paradisal island? Above all, why make them listen to the seductive voice of a cynical dropout who sees nothing but phoniness wherever he looks?

I wanted to say, Look, Barr—literature is not a Hallmark card with a message of hope and uplift: *You're a teenager now, but you'll get well soon.* Its purpose is not to help schools produce the next generation of well-adjusted hedge fund managers and corporation lawyers. No doubt the board of the Dalton School, where Barr had been head, was well staffed with managers and lawyers who saw the replication of themselves as the true subtext of whatever Dalton's mission statement happened to say about love of learning for its own sake. And no doubt Barr, serving at the pleasure of such a board, had absorbed its members' outlook and given it the kind of deft literary spin suitable to a think-piece in the *Times Book Review*.

Still, the piece did make me think. I thought about my own first reading of *Catcher*, during a blue period in my freshman year in college—how plaintively that voice had channeled and amped up my own cynicism, validated my comfortable, self-satisfied suspicion that much of life was a fraud. In my gloomy second-floor dorm room with winter's early darkness falling on the traffic in the street below ("January, 1962," my old bookplate says), I had sat in bed and underlined the good parts and joined enthusiastically in Holden's contempt for the secret slob Stradlater, the smarmy headmaster Thurmer, and the condescending Carl Luce.

I also remembered getting in trouble the first time I taught the book, at Prairie School. I had asked the students to write about their experience at Prairie, using Holden's voice. The gap between the Rotarian rhetoric of the school and the disintegrating world of 1968 seemed to make the assignment a natural. A girl's mother, emptying the wastebaskets, came across a draft that contained words like "goddam," "bastard," and "sonuvabitch." She let Jack Mitchell know that her daughter was being coached in vulgarity by her English teacher.

When Jack approached me about the matter, I had no trouble representing myself as the aggrieved party. Were the Bowdlers and Mrs. Grundy to be given their way with our texts? I had met at a conference some public school teachers from Iowa who reported that their district had mandated the excision by razor blade of a prurient passage in Steinbeck's *The Red Pony*—the passage in which a stallion becomes aware of the presence of a mare and bolts downhill to greet her, whinnying. The whinnying is all that Steinbeck chooses to describe, but its suggestiveness was evidently deemed too much for the boys and girls of Dubuque, who would perhaps be tempted to fill in the blanks from their own knowledge of farm life. Did Jack propose that I now take an X-acto knife to *Catcher*? What would be left of it but confetti if I did?

I believe that Jack, operating on a somewhat higher level of sophistication than the girl's mother or the Dubuque school board, was less concerned with niceties of word choice than with the indisputable fact that I had invited my students to compare his school to an educational backwater like Pencey Prep. Like murmuring about the unfairness of having to wear a celluloid collar, the assignment showed disloyalty to the institution that one served. As usual, however, he was gentle with me, and I resolved to keep my own counsel as to the most appropriate objects of my loyalty. I thought I owed it primarily to the truth, and I thought the truth was enshrined in exactly those kinds of literature that made students' parents and Jack Mitchell uncomfortable.

A year or so later, the girl whose mother had sifted her trash suffered a breakdown and had to be hospitalized. I visited her afterward in a halfway house, where I found her still blank-eyed and barely capable of conversation. Perhaps she had decided to check out like Holden Caulfield, but she had no story to tell.

"What we need," Kafka wrote, "are books that hit us like a most painful misfortune, like the death of someone we loved more than we love ourselves, that make us feel as though we had been banished to the woods, far from any human presence, like a suicide. A book must be the ax for the frozen sea within us." I took this as an article of faith when I was younger, actually copied it out and pinned it to my bulletin board in Madison, not stopping to wonder whether the prescription reflected an unhealthy morbidity on Kafka's part or to ask whether I accepted it so readily because of some unhealthy morbidity of my own. I still believe it, though I would now add that we equally need books that make us laugh out loud from the bottoms of our diaphragms, over and over again, as I did one night on a transatlantic flight while reading *Dave Barry's Guide to Guys*. It was the laughter of sheepish self-recognition—one of the most salutary kinds.

As to what books Holden Caulfield and his fellow high school students should read, the answer is "as many as possible." The chance that they will be harmed by any one book is slight, and slighter if they read and read and read. In any case, I find that most students, somewhat to my chagrin, are so far from being seduced by Holden that they dismiss him as a whiner and a loser, completely overlooking his troubled decency, compassion, and idealism; when I ask them to form an admissions committee and decide whether he should be given one more try, at Milton Academy, most of them turn thumbs down on having such a feckless schoolmate. If anything, the danger is that they are too wholesome, too uncritically committed to the myth of accomplishment and ascendancy, not that they are too alienated from it. When Lorrie Moore came to Milton to give a reading, someone asked her how to get an idea for a story. "Imagine the worst thing that could happen," Lorrie said. For weeks, the kids talked about her unforgivable negativity.

Even if students take a book seriously as a form of direct experience (most probably don't), and even if that experience makes them feel as if they were lost alone in the forest with night coming on, there are so many other books that promote so many other kinds of feelings. I tell my classes that literature is about trouble and that they should expect no less. But trouble is kaleidoscopic in form and sometimes beautiful in itself, and it does not always end badly. Even as bleak a journey as Cormac McCarthy's *The Road* (think: a man's severed head on display under a cake dome) delivers its young protagonist not to the cannibals that he and his father have been dodging from the start but to a family of survivalists who take him in.

In our encounters with trouble, however it ends, we discover the full range of what it means to be human, and to imagine that we could be human without encountering trouble is to engage in the worst sort of wishful thinking. The most comforting books (in the root sense: strengthening, like a fort) are those that look the gorgon in the face and stare her down. *You'll not turn me to stone—or, if you do, it will be the stone of integrity and endurance.* I think of James Baldwin's *Notes of a Native Son*, with its flintlike refusal to offer one iota of sentimental cover for the story of his father's death and his own racial embitterment. I think of Tobias Wolff, in *This Boy's Life*, insisting on his complicity with an adult abuser when he could easily and plausibly have represented himself as a pure victim. Any student who reads and understands these memoirs would have to be fortified by them—would have to feel more confident that even dark experience can be faced head on.

The very darkest of the dark, of course, is the realization that we are not the heroes we would like to think ourselves. One benefit of reading the *Odyssey*, above and beyond our pleasure in the marvelous proliferation of adventures, comes as we discover that the great man, the man of troubles whose long-delayed homecoming we root for, is actually a rather nasty piece of work. His name, in fact, derives from a verb that means "to give pain and to be willing to do so," and he travels the world giving exactly that—pillaging towns that have the misfortune to lie in his path, ruthlessly grinding a red-hot stake into the only eyeball of one adversary, sleeping with minor goddesses and leaving them in the lurch, and at last orchestrating the massacre of several dozen young men who might well have been forgiven, after his 20-year absence, for supposing him dead. Like the rest of us, Odysseus is a trouble-maker as well as a trouble-sufferer, an inseparable amalgam of sinner and saint.

If we accept some version of Kafka's take on the books we need, we quickly find that though it eliminates beach books and cheery treatises on the value of lessons learned in kindergarten, it leaves us with far more than we could ever read, let alone teach. In those tiny slices of time we are given with students, how do we choose what to assign, and how do we go about making the encounters as rich as we can—or at least avoid ruining them with clumsy or over-zealous efforts to enrich? Some of the books I was asked to read at Andover now seem to me, even allowing for shifts of taste in subsequent decades, to have been gross miscalculations. Yes, no doubt students should learn what an allegory is, and yes, *Pilgrim's Progress* is one, but very few ninth-graders, whether in 1957 or today, would find that its turgidities make a very effective psychological ice-ax. And what was Emory Basford thinking when he asked us, as sophomores, to plod for weeks through the flat wasteland of *Babbitt*?

Emory did better two years later when he laid on the great works of the American Renaissance. Here, clearly, was a reading experience worth wrestling with. Much of the time, in fact, it pinned me to the mat. My eyes would drift over several pages of *Walden* and at some point I would look up and realize that I hadn't understood a word. Emory, whose disdain for the trivialities of popular and commercial culture rivaled Thoreau's own, helped out by highlighting the more piquant lines in class. Mostly, what got me through was my admiration for him and his obvious reverence for the book. When I became a teacher myself, the reflex of that reverence brought me back to *Walden*, and I found that in the interim I had developed enough perspective to grasp both the text itself (at least to some extent) and the reasons why Emory had revered it. Whether I was able to teach it well—whether my students were simply sitting there and letting meaningless words slide by them—was another question altogether.

Reverence, though it did work in this case, is both an iffy teaching strategy and a questionable posture toward works of the imagination. It is the former *because* it is the latter. Students of the *Bible* have known for some time now that it is not a dictation by God but a human literary work—a loosely edited and morally anomalous one at that. Many of our cultural troubles today can be traced to those who still believe, against all evidence, that it is a dictation by God. On the other hand, we can derive all sorts of intellectual and emotional sustenance from the *Bible* if we approach it in a critical spirit. The same is true of *Walden* and of any other book. Students resist *Walden* for the same reason that they resist *The Catcher in the Rye*. They see in both an attack on what they have been led to believe is the most basic reason for going to school: to get ahead in life. Holden fantasizes about running away to a cabin in the woods. At first he thinks he'll take Sally, for the sex, but he soon realizes that her cynicism is only skin deep and that she's as conventional as any boosters clubber at heart. She doesn't want to go, and if she did they'd never get along. Thoreau lives out the cabin part. He doesn't have a candidate for the role of Sally but makes do by falling in love with a shrub oak, plaintively confiding to his journal, "There was a match found for me at last." This is weird and fascinating in its way (perhaps comparable to the "crumby stuff" that Holden sees going on in the windows of the hotel across from his) but not exactly a subject for reverence. Though I wish my students would be a little more skeptical about the world that Holden and Thoreau reject, I think it only fair that they should be equally skeptical about Holden and Thoreau. If they weren't resistant, they would not really be readers.

At Milton one of the courses we offer to juniors and seniors is a two-year sequence in English and American Literature—an old-fashioned tour of the (mostly white male) canon from *Beowulf* on up.

It draws hard-working literary types, those who might be reverence-prone, and part of the challenge of teaching it is to stave off reflexive genuflection. In they troop on the first day, bearing their copies of the *Norton Anthology*, that sanctified doorstop, ponderous and authoritative as any *Bible*. Before they settle in too comfortably with it, I have to subvert its authority. How does a work make its way between these covers, anyway? What if canonical works are no different from celebrities: famous simply for being famous? Stephen Greenblatt and his phalanx of sub-editors have an impressive array of credentials, but when it comes to reading they are just like you: they turn one page at a time. You are obliged, because you have chosen this course, to open yourselves to the works you find here, but each work is equally obliged to prove its worth to you. And so, on to *Beowulf*: is this a good poem, or merely an old one?

One school of thinking about how to approach the classics would say that it's a mistake to ask students to make literary judgments before they have had a chance to accumulate substantial literary experience. There are texts to be explicated, terms and techniques to be learned; there's a whole apprenticeship to be served before one is qualified to discern good from better from best. I recognize the logic in this position, and if our main goal were to train future candidates for the PhD in English I might actually agree. As I see it, though, our main goal is to nurture lifelong readers with a personal stake in what they read. Too many of the PhD's and would-be PhD's I met in graduate school had a professional stake but not a personal one: they needed to find a niche, however cramped and arid, that could sustain scholarly life, however crusty and lichen-like. By the time they were qualified to make judgments, they had lost both the motivation and the opportunity to judge. For a high school student, response is everything, and judgment is an inextricable part of response. Analyzing, he plays a necessary but often tedious academic game; judging, he establishes his independent existence as a reader. I am thrilled when Anna, one of my ablest explicators, frames her last paper of the year as a frontal assault on *The Scarlet Letter*. She writes about her high hopes going into the novel and about how quickly they crashed on its stilted language, heavy-handed symbolism, and tinny melodrama. Her own prose catches fire. The paper is not only her last but also her best.

Of all the writers whose pedestals we might encourage students to shake, Shakespeare heads the list. Bernard Shaw was onto something when he coined the term "bardolatry," a word that I introduce at the start of my Shakespeare course, along with the promise that we will not engage in it. Students are likely to begin a Shakespeare play with a toxic combination of attitudes, a compound of the bardolatry that has been preached to them in the past and their own perhaps experience-based expectation that what they'll be reading will be impossible to understand. What could be worse than having to pretend to worship the incomprehensible? The news that this writer has many obvious faults and that his plays contain many passages that *no one* can understand clears the air of both sanctimony and pretense and makes way for appreciation of Shakespeare as he actually was: a hard-working real-world dramatist who had to keep the turnstiles clicking and was quite willing to leave rough patches and loose ends in the current play in order to get on to the next one. (That his plays come down to us through the haphazard offices of a primitive and often incompetent publishing system is also an interesting part of the picture.)

The paradox at the center of teaching Shakespeare is that he is too great to *need* bardolatry. Why waste time denying or rationalizing the inconsistencies, the bombast, the tedious puns, and the lame plot devices (Hamlet is rescued by *pirates*?), when the plays repeatedly prove these weaknesses irrelevant by simply reaching out and seizing us by the scruff of the neck? They surmount their own slapdash origins like Prince Harry vaulting with ease onto his charger's back; and they are blithely indifferent to the rough handling of actors and directors, whose quest for original "concepts" can lead in what might seem to be unpromising directions. The *Romeo and Juliet* balcony scene turns out to play just as well in a swimming pool, and Richard III can plausibly scream for a horse when the jeep he is driving gets stuck in the mud.

Shakespeare was my own first literary love affair (not counting Hornblower and the space operas of Heinlein and Bradbury), and whenever I start teaching a play it is like renewing an old, old relationship, one that can be set aside and picked up again without a missed beat. Like most relationships, though, it is more complicated than it at first seems—or, at least, it has a history. The pure linguistic intoxication that I felt when I imbibed *Richard II* in the spring of 1958 is still with me, but many of the plays seem to have shifted shape over time. Today I can scarcely believe how much slack I once cut King Lear, how ready I was to accept his self-serving claim to be a man "more sinned against than sinning," and how I idealized the priggish daughter who is so hung up on telling the truth that she provokes a deadly familial war. When I watch Paul Schofield, in the Peter Brook movie, heave over a table in Goneril's refectory and send the plates and cutlery flying, I think that Schofield and Brook (and the Fool) have got it right: it's too bad this tantruming toddler became old before he became wise. Why ever did I choose to overlook such egregious bad behavior?

The play that has changed the most for me, however, is that ultimate canonical work, *Hamlet*, with which I became obsessed as a junior in college. I identified with the Prince, who seemed to me like a more romantic and more eloquent version of Holden Caulfield. I relished both his scathing tirades and his flippant repartee. Unlucky in love myself (or so I imagined despite having experienced nothing but the most rarefied crushes), I felt the full anguish of his rejection by Ophelia. His melancholy was an intoxicant, his anger a rush of righteousness. I scorned the distance that my teachers insisted was the proper stance toward a character in a literary work. When Olivier, sword in hand, leapt from a stone staircase to dispatch his uncle, I leapt with him. The existential laugh that Burton gave at the end, as he sank down on the vacant throne to let the poison do its work, seemed to come from my own mouth. That my goggle-eyed hero-worship of a character in a 350-year-old play might seem odd to the girl I took to the Burton film did not occur to me—or, if it did, demoted her in my mind to just one more pretty but uncomprehending Ophelia, who might better head straight for a nunnery than go on another date with me.

I first taught the play the year I was a Fellow at Andover. By way of mentoring, the chairman asked me to teach it not to my own students but to those of one of the senior department members, who would watch and offer suggestions. The teacher had little rapport with his class and was happy to sit back and let me do what I could, which was, by comparison with the enormous weight of meaning that *Hamlet* had for me, not much. By this time I had most of the text memorized, and I had spent an entire Christmas vacation gleaning nuggets of commentary from the variorum edition and inscribing them in the margins of my book. I was prepared to be both guru and drudge, but neither role seemed to have much effect. I talked and talked. When they talked— and they did so rarely—none of the students expressed anything like my affinity for the Prince. Their papers were dutiful but uninspired. After the last meeting, my would-be mentor complimented me on my knowledge of the play but had nothing to say about the non-event of my teaching it. His mentoring, like most I received in those figure-it-out-for-yourself days, was a non-event piled on a non-event. Mostly, he seemed dispirited at the prospect of having to take the class back on his own narrow shoulders.

My students today are often fascinated by *Hamlet* the play, though they have their doubts about Hamlet the character. I show them the 38 pages of notes that one web site coughs up on possible meanings of the phrase "smote the sledded pollax on the ice" and we share a laugh at the expense of X-treme literary scholarship. Then we get down to gauging the extent of our sympathy with the Prince. I am smart enough by this time to get out of the way and let the room fill up with the questions that Shakespeare's words naturally evoke. If a consensus emerges, it is rarely in favor of Hamlet. True, he's surrounded by insensitive adults and unsympathetic (and even treacherous) peers. True, he has some reason to believe that his uncle poured poison in his father's ear—and he *knows* that the drunken old goat has married his mother. But Hamlet talks too much and thinks too much. He's a habitual procrastinator—probably never turned his papers in on time back there in Wittenberg. If he wants revenge, he should get on with it and not let things fester. Worst of all, like Holden, he's too cynical, too ready to write off the world and all its juicy opportunities.

I'd like my students to like Hamlet a little more than they usually do. His philosophical questioning is appropriate to the age group, and so is his *weltschmerz*. But I can't help admiring their refusal to be swept along by the conventional assumption that he is a hero, and I have to love their reflexive faith that life must be more than a pestilent congregation of vapors. As for me, my identification with the Prince has weakened considerably over the years, and I even begin to feel a certain fellow feeling for Claudius. He is no better than he should be—indeed, a good deal worse—but he has been around the block often enough to understand that we must try to make our peace with living in a fallen state. This perspective, too, is a useful one for young and old to consider.

# Chapter 10

———✁———

# LOVE

*ADVISOR-INTERVENTION TIME AT the Cambridge School of Weston. At CSW, advisors are more important than teachers. They are the mothers with broad laps who swoop in to minister to skinned knees and hurt feelings. Very often the hurt feelings are the result of teachers who have not been sufficiently sensitive and affirming. Then the advisor-mother must convene a meeting to set things right.*

*As a teacher, I often feel like the defendant in these consultations, and it is so this morning with Jane and her advisor. Jane, an able but petulant student (what is it about CSW that seems to bring out the petulance in everyone?—it certainly brings out the petulance in me), has just scored a C on a paper and is unhappy about it. The advisor wants to open the subject of my relationship with Jane—whether I understand her or not, whether I appreciate her or not. She and Jane seem to share a negative presumption on this point.*

*"Jane," I say, when the probe's predictable direction has become clear, "my relationship with you isn't really what we need to be talking about. What we need to be talking about is the paper. The paper wasn't good—it didn't have a convincing argument, and it was full of grammatical errors."*

*Jane's eyes flash impatiently, as if I am trying to divert the conversation onto a sidetrack. "Thanks," she says, "I love you too."*

*"Jane," I say. "I love you. I love you, all right? But the paper wasn't good." Cambridge School has cultivated my stubbornness. A couple of years earlier, when I was first trying to figure out my way there, a girl had cried copiously when I returned her paper and I had raised her half a grade.*

I think, looking back on it, that Jane and her advisor had at least one leg to stand on. Much as I would have liked to tame the emotional maelstrom of CSW by objectifying kids' work, there can be no successful teaching without personal relationship, and "love" is as good a name for that relationship as any. Love, of course, comes in many shapes and sizes—so many that it is not always recognized as itself. I might have suggested that my blunt critique of Jane's paper was the surest evidence that I loved her as a teacher is supposed to love a student, but in the heat of the moment she probably would not have found this paradox persuasive, and who could blame her? "This hurts me more than it hurts you" is not an altogether persuasive line, and tough love is as often merely tough as loving.

How is a teacher supposed to love a student? We can more confidently answer the negative form of this question—how is he *not* supposed to? He is not supposed to violate the rules of decency (not to mention the statutes!) by taking sexual advantage of the fact that he is older and occupies a position of authority. That this apparently cast-iron principle has often been treated as a permeable membrane comes as no surprise. One can think of certain colleges where flouting it became a well-established counter-principle and aging professors moved with a blithe sense of entitlement through a series of younger and younger student wives until they might find themselves being spooned their pabulum in retirement by a justifiably resentful 26-year-old. In high school the taboos are stronger and their breach is less frequent and less systematized. But few administrators get through a career without having to prosecute cases—or, as they until quite recently tended to do, to sweep cases under the rug. I even recall a notorious instance where an administrator himself *was* the case and managed to walk away unscathed to an administrative job at another school.

For anyone other than a very young teacher, whose boundary- hopping might claim the excuse of some irresistible biological tug, these transgressions represent a form of professional suicide—not so much because they may be exposed and punished by exile as because they actually do violate the trust on which the work is founded. Standing *in loco parentis*, a teacher can no more justify a sexual relationship with a student than a parent could with a child, nor expect that such a relationship would be satisfying in any but the most transient and furtive way. Nevertheless, only the obtuse or disingenuous would deny that there is an erotic charge in teaching—a musical accompaniment that starts out as pulsing hard rock when you are only a year or two older than your students are and diminuendos over time into the muted but still perfectly audible and charming strains of a baroque chamber group. The children are beautiful, you have no choice but to look at them, and you would need to be made of stone not to be moved by their beauty. This pleasant perquisite must be enjoyed privately; it can never be mentioned. We all cringe at the tale, perhaps apocryphal but often repeated by administrators as a warning, of a teacher who somehow missed the feminist revolution and wrote a comment lauding one pupil's sparkling blue eyes. He should have enjoyed the sparkle and been smart enough not to commit his enjoyment to paper. Of course the sparkle was irrelevant to the girl's ability to parse a sentence or explicate a text, topics suited to public discourse. It was there just for him, a freebie, morning light on lake water, and he had to spoil it by putting words on it.

The physical beauty that surrounds a teacher continues to surround him as he himself becomes bald and paunchy and acquires an artificial knee or a mouthful of costly gold crowns. It renews itself like a garden of annuals timed for September instead of May. Here they come again, but I am the same I (an older, more battered version) and they are not the same they. I often wonder how old I seem to them. Not so old that they takes pains to avoid jostling me with their bookbags as they pour mindlessly up or down a stairwell. Once, though, when I was in my late 50's, a student asked to talk to me for a project he was doing for his Latin class. They had been reading Cicero's *De Senectute*, and the assignment was to interview an elderly faculty member on the subject of old age. I considered myself miscast but agreed. "How does it feel," the boy wanted to know, "to be so near death?"

The ingenuousness of this question, its utter lack of perspective and propriety, is perhaps an example of youthful beauty that transcends the physical. In fact, the physical beauty would be as bland and empty as the faces in some other school's yearbook if it were not attended by the qualities that bring it to life—qualities like energy, playfulness, and a voracious appetite for experience. Much as we enjoy their physical beauty, the young cannot helpfully model it for us: our hair thins and our paunch persists in expanding no matter how beautiful they are. What they can do is model those other attributes, the ones that are special to youth but remain open to any age. The young can be inspiring company for the old. When I feel sluggish and used-up of a morning, I look to them for a salutary jolt. When I sense myself slipping into a stodgy routine, I invite them to help me make a game of it. When I start thinking that there's nothing new under the sun, they remind me that I'm wrong. For these gifts I thank them and love them.

Concurrent with loving there is being loved. This too may be counted as one of the perquisites of the job, though we cannot depend on it with the same assurance that we can depend on seeing a few pairs of sparkling blue eyes every day. Being loved is a likely consequence of another of youth's attributes, the capacity for idealization (which often works in tandem with its opposite, the capacity for demonization). Just as kids are realizing that their parents are not the gods and goddesses they seemed in childhood, we show up to occupy the newly vacant pedestals. Perhaps we are funnier than dad or less embarrassing than mom—the particular qualifications matter less than the fact that we are there and available for pedestal duty.

A pedestal is both a seductive and a precarious spot. One can hardly *not* enjoy being idealized, but it entails temptations and dangers that can easily lead to breakage. Woe to the teacher who becomes enamored of his reflection in the blue eyes of his students and enrolls as a participant in his own charismatic myth. I think of Joe Roberts, a colleague during my first year at Prairie School. Joe was only half a decade older than I was but infinitely more experienced and self-confident. He already had a wife and two children, and he blended a stocky muscularity with a forceful exuberance that was hard to resist and that few students even thought of resisting. I idealized him myself and began to spend much of every weekend with him and his family. On Sunday afternoons we would watch the football game together and drink beer and discuss the deficiencies of the Prairie administration, which he, a graduate of über-progressive Antioch College, found at least as retrograde as I did. His wife Deborah, who had also been to Antioch but had a gentler and calmer personality, was patient with our nonsense. Eventually she would cook us dinner, ministering with little fuss to the boy still in diapers, the precocious five-year-old daughter, the husband fizzing with passionate animus, and the star-struck hanger-on.

Nominally hired as a social studies teacher, Joe made his primary emotional investment elsewhere. He was a superb athlete, as I repeatedly found out when I tried to compete with him. My training at Andover as Mr. Club did not prepare me for the inside head-fake—hardly more than a quick darting of the eyes—that he laid on in a touch football game one afternoon before accelerating around me and down the sideline for a touchdown. At tennis we were more evenly matched, partly because I had become a reasonably good player and partly because he sometimes threw his shoulder out; but even then he would serve underhand and win. He was, in fact, enormously competitive, and his all-in drive to come out on top made an interesting contrast with his professed belief that education should not be about competition but about cooperation and self-fulfillment.

Where he at least seemed to bring practice into line with ideology was in the gymnastics program that he pioneered at the school. Like soccer, which had been established as the main fall sport because Prairie was too small to field a football team, gymnastics was foreign to the Wisconsin kids who, if they paid attention to sports at all, doted on the Green Bay Packers, then in their glory years. But Joe burned like a blowtorch through layers of unfamiliarity and indifference. He set up his trampoline in the brand-new gym, drew a crowd, opened with a riveting lecture on the dangers of this equipment—how a boy he knew had approached it cavalierly and ended up dangling from a hook on a wall 20 feet away. Then, having raised an appropriate level of suspense, he climbed up there himself in his nifty stretch pants and sleeveless top and executed a high-altitude series of tumbles and twists. Hardly had his feet touched the floor again (a flawless dismount!) before he had two dozen girls signed up and eager to get started.

The gymnastics that Joe taught was in fact non-competitive: there were no other schools in the neighborhood with gymnastics teams to compete with, and even if there had been, the aim of his teaching was not to train you to rack up more points than a girl from Sheboygan or Fond du Lac. The aim—a fine one—was to help you gain control over your own body and discipline in your life. Girls flocked to this promise and flocked to it the faster because handsome, dynamic Joe, who seemed to embody control and discipline, was the one delivering it. He was strict and demanding but in a way that made you know he was on your side. He had perfected the affectionate bark, the mock-grudging concession of praise, the steady guiding hand. I, who had at that point perfected little and often had to operate on sheer bravado, learned a lot about teaching from watching him at work.

And then, at the end of my first year at Prairie—his first year, too—Joe was gone. He never told me and I never learned exactly what had happened. I believe the decision was his, for Jack Mitchell, as I knew very well, was not apt to fire anyone for insubordination. Perhaps Joe made some programmatic demand that Jack was not willing to meet and then felt obligated to walk away. But the conflict was not really about any practical matter; it was about irreconcilable personality types, the charismatic and the anti-charismatic. Jack, all bluster and hype, never spoke without a preliminary throat-clearing so grand that we gave it a name: the Phlegm Shift. His language had all the appeal of a Hubert Humphrey keynote address to the Future Farmers of America. Though generous with minor transgressions, he believed that authority was purely a matter of one's position in the chain of command. Joe, on the other hand, exercised the authority of physical presence and spiritual force—an authority that one could not derive from any standing in the hierarchy but had to win for oneself. It was also a kind of authority that depended on being idealized by others. Jack, unlikely to be idealized, didn't much care what the faculty and students thought of him: he was, after all, the headmaster. Joe enjoyed a little too much the gleam of unalloyed admiration in a girl's eye as she bent eagerly toward him to hear his review of her routine.

It was 1968, a year of charisma in which we could imagine for a moment that hierarchical authority was on its way out. We had already had the Summer of Love, and now we might look forward to the School of Love, where guru teachers and their disciples made magical learning as they went, without interference from people in offices. But no—the center held and the system remained intact. As Humphrey and his party regulars shortly afterward crushed the insurgent candidacy of Gene McCarthy, so Jack maneuvered the insurgent Joe out the door. I stayed, half hoping to inherit Joe's guru mantle (though I would certainly have broken my neck in the first five minutes on a tramp, as I had already so nearly done on the cargo net). The other half of me was beginning to suspect that charisma and its attendant idealization are an insufficient basis for organizing a school and, whatever egotistical pleasures they afford, not even a great way for an individual teacher to approach his work with students.

A better model, one that still features a kind of love as its motif, is the daily gathering of a class around the Harkness table. The very circularity of the arrangement repudiates a guru-based system. Where would the Great One sit? Instead it invites participation aimed at an imaginary spot in the center, a spot called the common good. Merely to enter a room arranged this way is to hear a message that has all but disappeared from our national life—the message that the best thing we have going for us as people is our generous responsiveness toward others and the solidarity that grows from it. When everything but the fire hydrants is being privatized (and we may shortly see corporate logos on them, too), we need to remind ourselves that there is even such a thing as "the common good."

In private schools like the one I teach at, competition and self-interest are often the subtexts of behavior. We preach constantly that learning should be an end in itself, and in these homilies we are sincere, partly because for us teachers it has been exactly that. And yet. Kids' families competed to earn the ever-rising sums required for tuition, room, and board. Kids competed with other kids for admission, and once in they continue to compete for grades because their voyage through a life of striving has barely begun. Much of what we do together is shadowed by the grim knowledge that, when the iceberg hits, there will be a limited number of places on the lifeboat pulling away toward the Ivy League.

Fortunately, teenagers are susceptible to idealistic messages, even messages that are not dependent on the charisma of the messenger. They are mostly willing to believe that literature may be a source of wisdom and that learning to express yourself accurately and pungently has an intrinsic value quite apart from its utility in the college application essay or the board room. Best of all, they tend to be interested in each other's ideas, appreciate each other's personalities, enjoy each other's company. They are open, in short, to an appeal to solidarity, regardless of the current that is flowing in the opposite direction. I make that appeal, explicitly, at the start of every year. We will succeed only to the extent that we succeed together, so it runs. Put your thinking out there where it can nourish others. Speak, listen, respond, and we will make something that didn't exist before and that belongs equally to all of us. When the ebullient Louis, at our last class meeting in June, says, "I think we achieved some pretty great solidarity" and the others nod, I feel that whatever the inevitable loose ends we're leaving, we've done the most important thing. Should we call it "love"? Perhaps not, but I can't think of a better word.

If literature really is a source of wisdom, a particularly rich trove of it resides in Virginia Woolf's *To the Lighthouse*. Whenever I lose my focus on creating solidarity and find myself tempted instead to connive in what might be (yes, please!) a student's incipient idealization of me—or conversely, whenever I feel that I have lost my touch and am coming across as a mere pedant or a bullying taskmaster, I remember a passage near the end of this great novel. The two teenagers, Cam and James, are finally making the boat trip to the lighthouse, a trip that stormy weather had denied them ten years earlier. When they wanted it then, their father had sternly decreed that the sea was too rough; now the old man is determined to go and take them with him, and they—being teenagers—come along resentfully, experiencing him as a tyrant who is coercing them into the ruin of a beautiful day. As they trail behind him on the way down the beach to the boat, they make a silent compact of resistance: yes, they will come, but they will do so sullenly, offering him no shred of what he wants from them.

The tools of Mr. Ramsay's coercion are a formidable mix of fatherly authority and childish vulnerability. A rigorous thinker and master of practicalities, he constantly prompts James to steer properly and instructs the dreamy, disoriented Cam on the points of the compass. What he wants most, however, is sympathy—for having grown old, for having lost his wife, their mother, who had been a bottomless well of sympathy for all of them before her death. Now he is a pest, fishing plaintively for connections to his children and muttering morbid lines from a poem about a castaway. He is like a teacher who has lost his touch and sits there helplessly amid a stony silence.

What he cannot do—what would make him feel better if he could—is read the children's minds. For though James remains intransigent, remembering his sainted mother and hoping mercilessly that the breeze will fail and his father's plans will be thwarted, Cam's monosyllabic replies to the old man's probes conceal a great tenderness and admiration for him. She thinks of how she looked up to him as a small child when she would enter his study and see him reading the newspaper with his friends, and she feels an aching wish to loosen her tongue and respond to his advances. And when they arrive at last at the lighthouse and Mr. Ramsay offers James a curt but congratulatory "Well done!" for his helmsmanship, Cam sees that even her brother, despite his impeccable mask of resistance, savors the praise and is won over. Both want to say to their father, "Ask us anything and we will give it you." Mr. Ramsay cannot know what they are thinking but must feel that they have yielded; Woolf tells us that he leaps "lightly like a young man" onto the shore.

No one has captured better than Woolf the ebb and flow of feeling between the generations, a tidal wash that every teacher who is listening can hear beneath the daily business of his class. However we might wish that students idolize us or fear that they despise us, the truth will be more complex than either of those things and more evanescent, as mutable as the pull of the moon.

The Cambridge School again, June, 1981—graduation day. It is my graduation day too: I have pulled myself together and gotten a job at Milton Academy, which will start in the fall. That, I think, will be my last stop as a teacher. Perhaps teaching is not my métier after all—my ongoing unease at CSW has forced me to ask the question. Should I, as the Harvard career office has suggested, look into managing money for a non-profit organization? This sounds better than bartending, and having never earned more than $12,000 in a year I am confident that

I could handle the non-profit part. But I remember how lovingly I was taught, and I want to give the profession one more try before I throw it over. Milton has offered me the chance. As things turn out, I will stay there for more than 30 years.

But now, on this nice spring morning, the future is as opaque as it always is, for the graduates and for me, and we have a ceremony to conduct. CSW offers few decorous occasions, but graduation is one of them. It's true that students in the back rows can be seen slipping out of their seats and into the gym for a celebratory slug or toke, but the sun is warm, the quad is green, Pachelbel's canon breathes serenity, and the substance abuse is not my problem. I remind myself that graduation is also known as commencement and that it proffers to all of us the fragrant bouquet of a fresh start.

One of the traditions here is that diplomas are handed out not by the head of school or the board chairman but by teachers. Each teacher comes forward, the head calls graduates' names at random, they step up to get their scrolls. In a school so given to histrionics, these transfers often take the form of extreme emotional displays, embraces so passionate and prolonged that an observer from the Legion of Decency might be tempted to intervene. When my turn comes, though, I don't expect to be caught *in flagrante*. I have loved teaching many of these children, but I have also worn my ambivalences on my sleeve. Now I am leaving, and I imagine that my well-known disaffection with the place will be a constraint, an awkwardness. Still, things go all right. Linda stands on tiptoe to give me a warm hug. Michele, in exchange for her diploma, hands me the flower she is carrying. Others accept handshakes amicably enough. My quota is all but filled when the head calls one more name.

"Stephen Drukman."

A ripple of anticipation passes through the audience. Though I've never taught him, "Ducky" Drukman and I have a history. A few months ago, in pique at the many laxities of CSW, I published a Swiftian satire in the school paper, a modest proposal for abolishing such repressive and authoritarian measures as lunch lines. Why not, I asked, just let everyone elbow his way to the trough as best he could? Though I believe that he did not fully grasp the irony, Steve Drukman correctly interpreted the piece as a criticism of his school and fired off an indignant riposte in the next week's paper. When I attempted to talk things over with him, he was not what you would call receptive.

Now he approaches the dais with a golden opportunity for some contemptuous gesture, something to send me packing. I brace myself and extend my hand in conciliatory fashion but he blows right by it. Before I can adjust, he has placed his hands on either side of my face and planted a fervent kiss square on my mouth. There is a roar of applause and laughter. A photo of the moment shows him headed back to his seat, grinning triumphantly and clutching the diploma that I have somehow managed to turn over to him, while kids in the background convulse in hilarity. No doubt I color a little. I am the butt of the joke, but it is a joke that I, too, can enjoy—not a boot in the backside but a kind of humorous amnesty, a re-establishing of perspective, a perfect send-off. Ducky kissed me. I am pretty sure he doesn't love me, but I have come to understand that when you choose to be a teacher, ambivalence is sometimes as good as it gets; and his kiss propels me into the uncharted future with a smile on my face.

# ACKNOWLEDGEMENTS

The members of my family, to whom this book is dedicated, have been with me all the way; and my students, whether mentioned individually or not, all taught me something. I especially want to thank these friends for reading the manuscript and encouraging me to get it out there: David Britton, Pat and Alan Cantor, Pam Cook, Richard Dey, Sarah Garraty, Josie Hughes, Natalie and Mark Schorr.

CPSIA information can be obtained
at www.ICGtesting.com
Printed in the USA
BVHW03s1827140218
508159BV00001B/33/P